66 – 12724 (2-9-69)

ESSAYS IN
POLITICAL SCIENCE

ESSAYS IN
POLITICAL SCIENCE

Edited by Edward H. Buehrig

INDIANA UNIVERSITY PRESS

BLOOMINGTON & LONDON

CONTENTS

PREFACE

In 1829 the Reverend Andrew Wylie, D.D., became Indiana University's first President, joining two other professors already on the ground—for instruction had actually begun in 1824. To a course of study that continued to be dominated by Latin and Greek, and that also contained English composition, mathematics, natural science, and evidences of Christianity, President Wylie, with the active concurrence of the Board of Trustees, introduced the first curricular reform. The school's announcement in the fall of 1829 (a "catalogue" of three pages) contained an innovation; the senior year was to include Moral and Mental Philosophy, Political Economy, and the Constitutions of the United States and of the Several States. These courses Wylie himself taught. By 1838 he had added two more, Moral Science and International Law.

Such were the beginnings of social science, but more particularly political science, at Indiana. In 1854 formal courses in history were introduced. The organizational device of the academic department came still later. The Department of History and Political Science first emerged in 1885.

Nearly thirty years later, on March 23, 1914, the Board of Trustees authorized the establishment of a separate department of political science. Professor Amos S. Hershey, who was to become its first chairman, had already in 1906 urged the division, concluding a letter to the Board with this rationale:

> . . . I would urge that Political Science has a right to be considered a separate and distinct science. It is so regarded in many of our leading Universities in this country and is made the subject-matter for a degree in Germany. A national Political Science Association was organized several years ago distinct from the American Historical Association and the experiment has been a decided success. While the close connection of Political Science with History on the one side and with Political Economy and Sociology on the other side is generally recognized, it is also generally felt and believed that Political Science has a distinct character of its own and that it differs from Historical Science in scope, purpose, and method. In scope it differs from History in that it concerns itself solely or mainly with the State and with Government as such, i.e. its subject-matter is more limited and specific than is that of history. Its specific purpose is the scientific study of Government, i.e. of legislation and administration, and, while it utilizes the results of historical investigation, it attempts to reach conclusions and generalizations of its own. Its method is comparative and to a certain extent philosophical instead of being purely historical, i.e. documentary. In these latter respects it bears a much closer resemblance to the allied sciences of Political Economy and Sociology than it does to History.

The lectures contained in this volume were delivered at Indiana University in the fall of 1964 in commemoration of the fiftieth anniversary of the Department, whose name meanwhile, in 1934, had been changed to Government. We are indeed grateful to the lecturers for their fine effort on our behalf. We wish also to acknowledge the financial assistance so generously given by the Indiana University Foundation.

EDWARD H. BUEHRIG
Chairman of the Anniversary Committee

ESSAYS IN
POLITICAL SCIENCE

The Use of Theory
in the Study of Politics

ANATOL RAPOPORT

Theory has not only many uses but also many meanings. It will serve the purpose of this discussion to examine some of these.

In the vernacular, "theory" frequently means a hypothetical reconstruction of events. For example, the police may entertain one or more theories about who committed a particular crime and how. The crucial feature of this kind of theory is an account of conjectured events, of which the observed events are likely consequences. For instance, a lipstick-stained cigarette stub found at the scene suggests that a woman was present, because the presence of a woman makes the presence of the lipstick-stained stub a likely consequence.

It is well understood that a theory of this sort is corroborated if events "fall into place," as it were. Contrariwise, the theory is refuted or at least weakened by evidence that contradicts the hypotheses of the theory. Such a theory is consequently falsifiable. It is noteworthy that this popular conception of theory (as falsifiable) comes closest to the meaning of theory in natural science. In natural science, too, a theory is a system of interrelated

3

hypotheses and deductions, a framework, into which specific observations are supposed to fit. Each time an observation is consonant with the hypotheses and their consequences, the framework is strengthened and vice versa.

Next, we note that in the behavioral, particularly in the social, sciences application of the term "theory" is not confined to falsifiable theory. Some expositions offered as theories by social scientists are not falsifiable. People who judge theories by natural-science standards declare such expositions not to be theories at all. For example, some such expositions are *normative*; that is, they describe states of affairs as they ought to be rather than as they supposedly are. Some other discussions offered as theories are essentially *taxonomies*—i.e., systems of classification—which in the last analysis reduce to definitions rather than to assertions, and so are not falsifiable.

Clearly, arguments about what ought to be properly called a theory are futile. It is much more instructive to look at the genesis of various types of expositions and discussions offered as theories and to examine the role they play in the development of social science, particularly of political science. By "political science" I mean the systematic study of politics and the ideas that emerge from such study.

NORMATIVE POLITICAL THEORIES

Political theory in the sense of a systematic formulation of political concepts is very old. Aristotle's writings contain complex theoretical notions about politics, and there are even older examples. In the Book of Kings, the prophet Samuel attempts to dissuade the Israelites from organizing the twelve tribes into a monarchical state. Samuel points out to the Israelites the undesirable concomitants of monarchy, such as taxes, military con-

4

scription, and labor conscription: "This will be the manner of the king that shall reign over you; he will take your sons, and appoint them unto him, for his chariots, and to be his horsemen. . . . And he will take your daughters to be perfumers, and to be cooks, and to be bakers. . . . And he will take the tenth of your seed . . . the tenth of your flocks. . . ." Samuel had a normative theory of government, according to which tribal organization was preferable to monarchy.

Aristotle in his typical Aristotelian fashion offered a taxonomy of political systems, such as oligarchies, tyrannies, and democracies; and in a manner less picturesque than Samuel's but more analytically profound, he argued the advantages and disadvantages of each. In both the Greek and the Roman world sophisticated constitutional arrangements were spelled out in great detail and frequently supported by theoretical arguments purporting to explain the functions of the arrangements.

All these are examples of normative political theory. So is the Divine Right of Kings. This doctrine, although it *sounds* like an assertion of a fact—namely, that the king's power derives from a mandate given by God—is nevertheless an assertion of a value—namely, that the legitimacy of the king's power *should not* be challenged by mortals. Finally, our own system of government is based on a normative theory, implied in the principle of checks and balances, which stems from the notion that "concentration of power" is undesirable, which in turn stems from the idea of so-called natural rights.

A normative theory is not falsifiable. If facts are marshalled as evidence that a political system does not fulfill the ends for which it was designed, it is always possible to blame the machinations of opponents, or degeneration of mores, or dereliction of duty, or unforeseen circumstances. The *theory* can always be absolved, because a normative theory asserts not what is but

5

what ought to be, and since what ought to be hardly ever occurs, a normative theory is never actually put to a test.

As is well known to students of political science, there has been a strong reaction, starting in the twenties or thirties and particularly in the United States, against normative political theory. This reaction was not confined to political science but pervaded all disciplines with claims to scientific status. The philosophical justification of this reaction is expressed as a system of thought known as logical positivism or logical empiricism. This outlook places great emphasis on verifiable data as the ultimate source of all knowledge. This view in itself is hardly controversial. However, the real punch in the typical logical-positivist critique of all theoretical formulations is in its insistence on justifying the *meaning* of every concept or assertion by clear-cut connections with observable data. Thus the logical positivist not only asks "How do you know?" every time some generality is asserted; he also asks "What do you mean?" He impugns not only the credibility of assertions but also their meaningfulness.

Practically the entire verbal output of social science, in particular of political theory, can be and sometimes is declared to be meaningless by the logical positivist, pending definitions of terms. Moreover, the logical positivist demands not formal, dictionary definitions but definitions that *extensionalize* the concepts—that is, point out their observable referents.

Thus the logical positivist would insist that before an assertion like "The preservation of democracy necessitates curbs on concentration of power" can be fruitfully discussed, one needs to establish the meanings of the key terms, "democracy" and "power." Moreover, purely taxonomic definitions, no matter how

6

convincing or elegant they sound—such as "Democracy is government by the people"—simply will not do. They point to no unambiguously observable referents.

The constructive aspect of the logical-positivist critique manifests itself in the notion of the operational definition. Such a definition indicates the observables, which give the concept defined specific empirical content. The operational definition has become a hallmark of "hard science." Its overwhelming importance was demonstrated in the 1920's through the conceptual analysis of the ideas underlying the theory of relativity. It became clear that neither the spatial distance between two points nor the time interval between two events is definable unless one takes into account the measurement procedures used to determine the length of the distance or interval; but when these are taken into account, it turns out that distances and time intervals, heretofore intuitively accepted as objective and independent facts, actually depend on the point of view of the observer and are themselves interdependent.

From the 1920's on, the operationalization of concepts and the emphasis on objectively verifiable data became practically synonymous with science. The manifestation of this attitude in psychology was the behaviorist doctrine. Sociology, too, in the United States soon became predominantly a compilation of data with statistical analyses attached. The positivist attitude in law was embodied in the operational definition of law as *that which the courts in fact decide,* a concept advanced by Oliver Wendell Holmes and later by Jerome Frank and by Felix Cohen.

In the spirit of the times, the empirical attitude became pronounced also among the political scientists—particularly in the United States, where empiricism flourished in a climate characterized by a predominantly pragmatic outlook on life.

The antitheoretical bias of Americans is proverbial; and this bias reveals itself even in academic pursuits, where theory in its most general sense of abstract and general discussion of concepts might be expected to enjoy great prestige. Although, as should be clear, knowledge divorced from theory is not worth the name, emphasis on data and a reluctance to draw general conclusions characterize a great deal of research in the United States, not excluding research related to politics. As we have seen, the tendency can be viewed as a manifestation of positivism, which has pervaded many disciplines. It can also be traced to a growing skepticism toward the pieties of normative political theory. Positivism in the study of politics juxtaposes the "realism of facts" to the "idealism of theory." To the pragmatist, "theory" is almost synonymous with sterile speculation.

THE HYPOTHETICO-DEDUCTIVE METHOD

It is not true, of course, that theories are constructed *in vacuo*. Every theory emerges from some conscious or unconscious generalization of observations or at least of impressions. Nor are there such things as "bare facts." Every assertion of fact is based on (often tacit) theoretical presuppositions. It is instructive to recall that in earlier times the battle between rationalists and empiricists raged in natural philosophy. At one end stood the system-builders like Plato, Hegel, Descartes, and Schelling; at the other, the proponents of naked empiricism like Francis Bacon. What is today conventionally known as "the" scientific method is a synthesis of rationalism and empiricism, the so-called hypothetico-deductive method of physical science.

The empirical component of this method is reflected in the dictum that truth, indeed the meaningfulness of every assertion, depends on certain correspondence rules which connect the assertion to observations—characteristically, *future* observations.

8

This is the criterion of truth based on verifiability and predictability. The rationalist component of the hypothetico-deductive method is reflected in the way assertions are related to one another. The assertions do not form a mere assembly or catalogue of facts, as they would if each were a summary of an independent set of observations. Rather, the assertions are connected by chains of deduction, in which one is a logical consequence of others. A theory, then, in the context of the hypothetico-deductive method, consists of a set of postulates or assumptions together with all the assertions that follow from these postulates in the course of strict logical deduction. In physical science and increasingly in biological science these deductions are typically carried out in mathematical language, since the grammar of this language is precisely the grammar of logical deduction formidably developed.

It should be noted that the requirement of empiricism—that is, the verification of assertions—needs to be applied, not at each link of a deductive chain, but only at the end. For example, Newton's law of gravity asserts that the attractive force between two particles in the universe is proportional to the products of the masses and inversely proportional to the distance between them. Obviously, this assertion cannot be verified directly. We cannot stretch a spring balance between the earth and the sun in order to measure the "attractive force" between them. The law of gravity is verified only through its *consequences,* among which are the shapes of the planets' orbits, the planets' rates of revolution, etc. These consequences are directly verifiable, and through these verifications the plausibility of the law is established. In this way, the hypothetico-deductive method incorporates the requirement of empiricism that the connection between assertions and observables must always be maintained and at the same time avoids the pitfall of crude empiricism: the demand that this connection be established at all levels of discourse, ignoring the role of theoretical deduction.

Whether the hypothetico-deductive method (which made the exact sciences what they are) can be extended to the social sciences has been a live methodological issue for some decades at least. In fact, the issue had already become explicit in the writings of Auguste Comte, the exponent of the positivist view of social science.

CAN NATURAL-SCIENCE METHODS BE
EXTENDED TO SOCIAL SCIENCE?

The pros and cons are easy to discern. The success of the hypothetico-deductive method is coextensive with the phenomenal success of natural science. The idea of extending the method to fields of knowledge dealing with man as well as with nature is an attractive one. On the other hand, the rigor of the hypothetico-deductive method severely limits the contexts in which it can be sensibly applied; these contexts must be in the realm of precisely specifiable, observable, and, above all, repeatable events. Such events are not absent from human affairs; but the difficulty is to establish connections between such events and the concepts that constitute the heritage of the social scientist, concepts that accumulated during the time when no one thought of applying operational standards to definitions, when the value of a definition was judged by its intuitive appeal or its elegance of expression rather than by the sharpness with which it singled out empirical referents.

There is a sure way of getting around this difficulty: choose objects of investigation in which events *are* clearly specifiable. This necessitates radical shifts of emphasis. One hunts where the ducks are; consequently, one is guided not by the perceived im-

10

portance of concepts or of research problems but by their tractability.

Some are willing to pay this price, and others are not. Here is the focus of the controversy. It divides the social scientists into the "hard" and the "soft." The former accuse the latter of muddleheadedness; the latter accuse the former of trivializing social science. Specifically, essays on the nature of politics, of law, of government, etc., do not arouse much interest in those who view politics as the totality of observable political events—e.g., elections, coalitions, lobbies, distribution of patronage, or the mechanics of legislation. On the other hand, a most detailed account of the workings of political machinery leaves the "soft" social scientist cold. He wants to know how the machinery came into being; what is likely to become of it; how it fits into the concept of man as the political animal; and, perhaps, whether it serves the goals of man and how.

If the "hard" political scientist is not satisfied with pure description, if he aspires to build a theory, the only tractable theories he can hope to construct at this time are those that deal with very narrow aspects of politics—e.g., the statistics of voting behavior or the formation of clearly discernible coalitions. These matters are far from the "soft" political thinker's foci of interest.

The issue between the "fact-oriented" and the "concept-oriented" students of politics involves more than a divergence of intellectual interests. It involves also a difference in outlook. One might ask why we should want to understand the working of political machines or of the forces that have given rise to them. Do we wish to control the machines and the forces? Or do we wish merely to be able to predict their behavior so that we can adjust ourselves accordingly? Or, perhaps, we would like to destroy the machines. The problems of obtaining knowledge and of applying it are not easily separated. Depending on their purposes, different persons will go after knowledge with different kinds of tools and so obtain different kinds of knowledge.

We see, then, that the issue between the positivists and their opponents cannot be resolved in a facile manner. The issue is not whether social science, in particular the study of politics, can be made fact-oriented and so "scientific" or whether it is destined to remain on the conceptual level and close to the humanities. Obviously, political science *can* be made "hard" by properly selecting the objects of study; but this is done at a price—namely, a disengagement from the traditional pattern of thought that has given rise to political theory. This price is deemed too high by many.

TAXONOMICAL THEORIES

If only the concepts that traditionally were considered relevant to political theory could be preserved and if, at the same time, they could be rigorously defined in accordance with operational standards, then, perhaps, one could have one's cake and eat it. In sociology, a great deal of effort has been expended in this pursuit. For example, the school of thought associated with Talcott Parsons brings to the foreground essentially problems of definition and of recognition. All such programs, in fact, are aimed toward the creation of a *taxonomy*. Their successful completion enables the "theoretician" to "diagnose" observed phenomena as members of theoretically established categories. Clearly, such programs succeed only to the extent of delineating entities to be talked about—i.e., the *subjects* of supposedly meaningful assertions. They do not touch upon the problem of determining what is to be said about the entities. They do not deal with the *predicates* of assertions. Recognition, not prediction, is the end product of systematic taxonomy.

12

Although recognition may be necessary for scientific theory as it is conventionally thought of, it is hardly sufficient. It is as if medicine were entirely confined to diagnosis, while problems of prognosis, prophylaxis, and treatment remained untouched. Or, to use another comparison, it is as if the theory of chess were confined entirely to the classification of openings, so that one never failed to recognize Queen's Gambit, Sicilian Defense, and other traditional openings. Obviously, the most faultless record in identifying such moves would not establish one as a competent chess-player.

So far, I have not said anything positive about the use of theory in the study of politics. The obvious uses of theory in the study of natural phenomena—namely, prediction and control—come readily to mind; but whether such uses of theory can be extended to politics or to any other field of human behavior is questionable, because of the enormous complexity of phenomena involving human behavior. Specifically with regard to control, a most peculiar problem arises, for the objects of political control are people. A science that enables some people to control others is not likely to develop if both the would-be controllers and the would-be objects of control have access to the relevant information. Keeping such information secret raises problems of another sort—namely, problems related to the ethics of science. Genuine science does not tolerate secrecy.

With regard to prediction, these problems do not arise; but others do—namely, the extremely limited scope of political behavior about which reliable theories with predictive power can be developed. This range of behavior comprises phenomena in which some measure of regularity is observed—for example, systematic fluctuations in voting behavior or in public opinion. If one confines oneself to these areas, one is never sure whether he comes to grips with the fundamentals of the political realm.

13

If one starts from the other end, as it were, by providing operational definitions for the traditional concepts, theory remains largely confined to taxonomic programs. Scholars involved in such programs simply do not get around to formulating verifiable propositions relating the concepts so defined, much less to organizing the propositions into a coherent deductive theory.

THE MODEL APPROACH

There is still a third approach to political theory, one that I believe to be promising and that I shall now describe. This is the so-called model approach. Please note that the concept of the model enters both the positivist's and the traditionalist's orientations, but "model" means something very different in each case. To the positivist a model is a rigorous description of observed events. If the positivist uses the hypothetico-deductive method, his models become simply the basic assumptions from which the observed events are to be derived by rigorous (usually mathematical) deduction. Thus, for example, in demography, the logistic model of population growth is a precise mathematical statement that relates the rate of growth positively to the size of the population attained and negatively to the square of the population. The degree of agreement between the time course so predicted and the observed time course constitutes the degree of corroboration of the model. Thus the positivists' models do not differ in any way from those by which the natural scientist explains phenomena.

The traditionalist also sometimes speaks of models; but in his formulation the models usually turn out to be analogical, metaphorical ones. For example, some theorists of international relations speak of "balance of power" and sometimes argue its pros and cons, both from the normative point of view (whether or

14

not "balance of power" is a good thing) and from the point of view of the usefulness of the concept in the study of international politics. Now the phrase "balance of power" readily brings to mind a number of things. Balance makes us think of scales; and power makes us think of force, pressure, or energy. All of these are, however, just words. If a positivist were to insist on an operational definition of "balance of power" or, for that matter, of "power," as it is used in this context, it is doubtful whether his demands could be satisfied. To be sure, one could *concoct* an operational definition in terms of calculable military potentials or what not; but obviously this is not what theorists of international relations have in mind when in their discourse they use the phrase "balance of power." The phrase encompasses much more that is intangible. It is the same with "checks and balances," a concept much used in describing the American political system.

Please note that by pointing out the lack of operational definitions of phrases like "balance of power" or "checks and balances" I am by no means impugning their importance. On the contrary, I am convinced that something that can be called "balance of power" did play a dominant role in European international politics for at least a century. I am also convinced that something that can be called "checks and balances" did play a vital role in shaping American political institutions. All I am saying is that concepts like "balance of power" or "checks and balances," sometimes offered by political theorists as examples of "models," do not qualify as models from the positivist's point of view, since they play at most a descriptive role. They have hardly any *deductive* potential.

This, incidentally, applies also to mathematical descriptions, no matter how accurate. For example, if we were to plot the time course of the per cent of the Republican vote in successive federal elections, we could conceivably describe the resulting curve by a

15

mathematical formula. Such a "formula" would by no means constitute a "mathematical model of voting behavior," since hardly anything could be deduced from it. On the other hand, if we made certain assumptions concerning factors influencing the vote and concerning their interdependence and from these assumptions *derived* the theoretical time course of the vote (which might or might not agree well with the observed time course), the assumptions would constitute a model of voting behavior.

In short, both the positivist and the traditionalist use models in their theoretical discussions. The positivist demands from his model above all *productiveness*—i.e., a deductive potential that will allow the theoretician to predict (or post-dict) events as deduced consequences from the model. Naturally the positivist would also like his predictions to agree with the observations. In other words, he seeks not only productiveness but also accuracy. The traditionalist, on the other hand, demands *suggestiveness* from his models. He seldom goes beyond description and classification in his treatment of events. A model serves for him as a link between the pattern of events observed and some familiar or commonplace pattern. Thus, the old-fashioned depiction of the state as a human body—with the head representing the kingship, the arms representing the armed forces, and so on—was a "model" in the traditionalist's sense, but of course could not qualify as one in the positivist's sense, being totally unproductive. Models like "balance of power" occupy an intermediate position. They may be to some extent productive. For example, if it can be established that England helped France whenever Germany became stronger and vice versa, these can be displayed as deductions from the "balance of power" model. But ordinarily the deductions of such metaphorical models are not far-reaching. They are typically only restatements of the observations that had suggested the model in the first place.

TWO NEW TYPES OF MODELS

I should like to propose some models for political theory that are like the positivist's in their construction but like the traditionalist's in their purpose. That is to say, the types of models I have in mind are *generated* perfectly rigorously—for example, mathematically—but the demand that these models be immediately compared with phenomena with the aim of corroborating or refuting them is not made. The purpose of such models is not primarily prediction (which is the positivist's concern); much less is it control (which is the pragmatists' concern); rather it is "understanding," which is the concern of traditionally oriented theory in social science. There is a proviso, however—namely, that criteria of understanding are to be rigorous, not merely intuitive. I hope that as I discuss some actual examples of such models, the meaning of this proposal and the basis for its possible justification will become clear.

I have in mind two classes of models that have already appeared on the horizon of political theory. The two classes differ widely in method and in spirit. They are alike in that both derive from rigorous quantitative assumptions, both use mathematical deduction, and both score rather low on the scale of verifiability and prediction; but both score very high, in my opinion, on the scale of conceptual enrichment, of which there will be more to say in conclusion.

The two classes of models I have in mind are the *system-theoretical* and the *game-theoretical*. The former is spiritually akin to the natural sciences and adapts from the latter the characteristic generalization of the notion of causality, which I shall discuss in a moment. In the formulations of system-theoretical models the traditional concepts of political theory, which derive

17

from notions intimately related to the content of politics (e.g., power, legitimacy, welfare), are all but absent. In their classical formulation the system-theoretical models are deterministic, like the models of classical physics. This, however, is not an inherent limitation. System-theoretical models can also be made non-deterministic by the use of stochastic assumptions. Nevertheless, they have the flavor of determinism in the sense that the properties of a *system* are assumed to be the determinants of events (whether categorically or probabilistically) and that these properties may have little or nothing to do with the inclinations or goals of the elements that are members of the system.

The other class of models, the game-theoretical, on the contrary, derives from theories of decision and therefore assigns an important role to the normative aspects of theory. In certain contexts, it is even possible to single out the "best" decisions, and it is generally assumed in the context of game-theoretical models that "perfectly rational" decision-makers will make such optimal decisions. But here, too, the scope of the models is not confined to this dominant aspect (in which "classical" game theory had been formulated). As we shall see, the inclusion of non-zero-sum games and N-person games necessitates the abandonment of normative theories and places greater emphasis on descriptive analysis.

THE SYSTEM-THEORETICAL APPROACH

The fundamental notion in the system-theoretical approach is, of course, the *system*. There are various definitions of "system," but in one respect they all agree. To speak of a system means to single out for attention first some population of elements or entities, next some variables in terms of which the entities are described, and finally some specified relations among the variables.

The *state* of a system is defined in terms of particular values assigned to the variables. A *dynamic* system theory is said to be complete if the designation of initial states of the system enables one to derive, by virtue of the specfiied relations, the time course of the system as a succession of states (categorically or probabilistically). A static theory of such a system requires only that equilibrium or steady states be specified, such that once a system finds itself in one of these it will persist in that state.

An extremely important notion related to static theory is that of stability of equilibria, or steady states. A stable equilibrium is one that obtains if accidental departures from the equilibrium state set in motion forces that tend to bring the system back to the equilibrium state; and an unstable equilibrium is one that obtains if an accidental departure sets in motion forces that carry the system even farther in the same direction. In the language of cybernetics, a stable equilibrium is characterized by negative feedbacks, whereas an unstable equilibrium is characterized by positive ones.

It is evident that these notions stem from the study of systems in natural science. For example, a system of chemical reactions is specified by the substances taking part in the reaction; their concentrations, pressures, temperatures; the permeability of the boundaries of the container; the nature of the surrounding medium (if the boundaries are permeable to matter or energy); and other variables. The relations are determined by physio-chemical laws. The states of the system are described by the concentrations of the various substances, their pressures, etc. Steady states are defined as those in which the values of all the relevant variables remain constant. Such steady states can be stable or unstable.

Exactly the same method can be theoretically applied in biology—for example, in population genetics or in ecology. The difference between the two fields of application is that whereas in chemistry the laws governing the interactions are known with great precision and the initial conditions can likewise be precisely specified, so that the task of deriving dynamic and static properties amounts simply to an application of mathematical techniques, in biology the laws of interaction can be stated with only questionable confidence and initial conditions can be determined only roughly.

A system-theoretical approach to any of the behavioral sciences—for example, economics, social psychology, sociology, or political science—would involve the singling out of elements and variables on the one hand and of the laws of interaction on the other. The former are at the present time matters of preference and choice (that to which one decides to pay attention). The latter are at the present time no more than guesses. The specification of initial conditions would be expected to be even more difficult in the behavioral sciences than in biology, especially if the variables selected for their relevance were only indirectly observable—for example, "inclinations to vote," "intensity of political pressure," "power." (Note that operational definitions may well be in terms of probabilities—i.e., quantities only indirectly observable. Operational definitions demand only that the notions defined be *ultimately* connected to events *in principle* observable.) Therefore, even if the task of *formulating* a system of interest in political theory were accomplished, the justification of this enterprise in classical terms—i.e., in terms of predictive power— would be extremely problematic. One simply cannot expect high predictive power from a theory for which elements were freely chosen on the basis of their presumed relevance and for which laws of interaction were also freely chosen, probably on the basis of their mathematical tractability.

If one cannot expect predictive power from system-theoretical models of interest to the political theorist, what good are these models? Their value is to be sought in their potential for enriching the conceptual repertoire of the theoretician and in their role as *steps* in the search for relevant variables and valid laws of interaction. In other words, the value of such models is heuristic: they contribute to the sophistication of the investigator even when he is a long way from a successful theory.

I shall cite an example that I have used on several occasions before. My excuse for so repeating myself is that it is a good example. A generation ago Lewis F. Richardson, a British physicist and meteorologist, constructed a mathematical model of arms races based on both positive and negative feedbacks. The positive feedbacks were embodied in the assumption that the rate of growth of armament expenditures by one power or power bloc was stimulated by the level of these expenditures by a rival power or power bloc. The negative feedbacks were embodied in the increasing burden of the armament expenditures. The result was a well-formulated system. The dynamics of the system were reflected in the theoretical time course of the total armament expenditures. By properly adjusting the parameters, Richardson succeeded in getting a perfect fit between the actual expenditures of the Entente and the Central Powers in the years preceding World War I and expenditures in the theoretical time course.

Now the significance of that fit is not great in view of the number of free parameters to be adjusted and the few points in the observed time course. However, as I have said, the value of system-theoretical models of this sort is to be sought not in their predictive power but in their heuristic value—i.e., in their suggestiveness. For example, in the construction of the model, Richardson was obliged to give meaning to "negative" armament expenditures. Since such quantities can have no inherent meaning, another quantity had to be proposed similar to armament expenditures but with a negative sign. Richardson proposed interbloc trade to play the part of this quantity (as an index of cooperation counteracting arms expenditures as an index of rivalry). The net index of hostility, then, became the algebraic difference between armament expenditures and trade volumes. Negative values of this index were interpreted as levels of co-operation; and positive levels as levels of hostility. It was in terms of these net values that the time courses of the indices were fitted. The interesting result was not the actual fit (the significance of which, as I have said, is small) but the by-product conclusion—namely, that the European "system" in the years 1908–14 was *unstable,* judging by the values of the estimated parameters. Had the combined armament expenditures of the powers been some five million pounds sterling per year smaller (or, equivalently, had the interbloc trade been larger by the same amount), the system might have gone into reverse—that is to say, toward ever-increasing cooperation (perhaps a United Europe) instead of to the runaway arms race and war.

At the risk of redundancy I repeat that this result is not to be taken seriously as a theoretical conclusion. There are too many assumptions and simplifications piled on one another in Richardson's model to make it a substantive theory of arms races, nor is there a way to test the intriguing conclusion concerning the "instability" of the European system before World War I. History is not replicable under controlled conditions. Note, however, that the basic ingredients of the theory make sense in present-day terms. Many students of international affairs are inclined to attribute great importance to the mutually stimulating factors in the development of the cold war, especially in its early escalating phases. Proposals have been made of deliberate steps designed to reverse the trend toward war. Since drastic steps, such as substantial unilateral reductions of defense expenditures, would be sure to be resisted by decision-makers who think in conventional power terms, small steps have been suggested on the assumption that, although they would in no way upset the power balance, they might instigate a self-perpetuating trend in the direction of releasing tensions and so pave the way for more substantial agreements. Whether or not one believes in the effectiveness of such steps, the underlying assumptions are at least intellectually respectable. Note, however, that such assumptions are based on qualitative common-sense arguments. In the system-theoretical approach such arguments are formulated in precise quantitative terms. To validate such arguments or to refute them data are needed. The end result of the model, then, is *an instigation to search for relevant data*. These data may be found in armament expenditures, or they may not. They may perhaps be found in the tone of diplomatic discourse, in trade volumes, in indices of geopolitical factors or of mass behavior. We do not know them a priori. Neither does the system-theoretical approach tell us where they are to be found. All that we learn is how to construct admittedly crude models of interaction to test various hypotheses of interaction. Nevertheless, crude as they are, such quantitative models are superior to the purely verbal catalogues of "causes and effects," for in real life causes and effects are intricately interlaced. Events and trends have different simultaneous effects, and some of these may be in opposite directions. On the verbal level this leads only to futile arguments about which effects are the important ones. The mathematical model, on the other hand, reflects the "counterpoint" of causes and effects and allows the assessment of the relative strengths of the effects and so of their resultants. Admittedly, this assessment is made on the basis of the deductions from the assumptions of the model; but at least the source of the deductions is clear. If the deductions do not tally with reality, one has at least an idea of how to modify the assumptions to make the deductions fit better.

The system-theoretical point of view, exemplified by Richardson's attempts to construct a mathematical theory of international conflict, is now reflected in a prominent sector of political theory. If we take into account the difficulty of drawing the line between political theory and other fields of social science, the importance of the system-theoretical approach appears even more pronounced, for this approach contributes most effectively to the breakdown of interdiscipline barriers. The system theorist, in selecting the entities and the variables relevant to his theory, does not inquire into their academic-disciplinary pedigrees. From his point of view there is absolutely nothing wrong about mixing in the same model entities and variables derived from political, economic, or psychological concepts. Thus it turns out that formulations inspired by system theory may be of prime relevance to political theory regardless of their discipline of origin, if any.

In the work of Karl Deutsch, for example, who carries a political-science union card, history, economics, and politics are intertwined with ideas derived from system theory and from communication engineering. The result is a heady mixture indeed. The outstanding value of this mixture is, as I have said, in its rich suggestiveness. By translating theoretical notions into quantitative terms wherever possible and by suggesting at least *possible* interrelations among the quantities so defined, system theory *points* to data to be gathered and, moreover, suggests how such data are to be related—i.e., instigates data-gathering with a purpose.

There are, of course, several levels of theoretical sophistication. Some of the ideas suggested by system theory may suggest nothing but "see whether this index is correlated with that index and to what extent." This is theory on a low level (but theory nevertheless). In its fully developed context, however, system theory may point not merely to correlations between pairs of indices but to complexes of intertwined relationships from which a truly powerful picture of gross political process may emerge. If this happens, system theory will have accomplished its aim.

We turn now to the other modern development in the realm of ideas that has been acclaimed as a great source of inspiration for political theory—namely, the theory of games. This approach was originally developed in the context of a theory of rational decisions, and was extended to situations in which the outcomes of decisions are controlled not by a single decision-maker but by two or more, whose interests (i.e., preferences for the outcomes) are typically in conflict with each other.

In this connection it is useful to recall that a theory of rational decision involves, of course, a definition of rationality. A systematic comparison of situations in which decisions are typically made reveals at once that the definition of rationality must vary with the situation. For example, if a decision-maker is faced with a definite range of alternative decisions (courses of action), and if he knows with certainty which course of action leads to what outcome, and, moreover, if he has a definite rank order of preference among the outcomes, there can be only one definition of "rational decision": the rational decision is that which leads to the most desirable outcome.

Suppose, on the other hand, the more realistic situation, in which each of the various decisions may lead to more than one outcome. Then the concept of rationality just defined does not apply, for although the outcomes may still be ranked according to preference, the decisions can no longer be so ranked. The same decision may lead to a good outcome or to a bad outcome. In this context the theory of rational decision is *extended,* for example, by the notion of the "expected utility" associated with each of the decisions. "Expected utility" makes sense if numerical values can be assigned to designate degrees of preference for the outcomes and if probabilities can be assigned to the various possible outcomes associated with each decision. Operations research is typically developed on this level. The fundamental problem of operations research is to find optimal values of certain controllable variables, given the constraints of the situation, often including probabilistic components.

So far we have assumed a single decision-maker, who controls certain variables. He may not control other variables, which may be determined by a "state of nature" (e.g., weather or statistical fluctuations of market prices); but whatever controls those variables is supposed in this context not to be guided by interests of its own. The weather, for example, is indifferent to the goals of the decision-maker. The stock market also is usually assumed to be affected by gross, impersonal factors.

As soon as another *rational* decision-maker enters the picture, we are in the realm of the theory of games. In this context the theory of rational decision purports to become a theory of rational conflict. It is not difficult to see why this conceptual genesis of the theory of games became a source of excitement in circles concerned with political theory. Certainly conflict is an important ingredient of politics and rationality is an important ingredient of theory. Almost by definition, therefore, the theory of games could be looked to as a source of fundamental theoretical ideas in the study of politics.

So it looks on the surface. A closer examination of game theory, however, reveals something else. In answer to the question "Is game theory useful in the study of politics?" the answer must be most emphatically "Yes and no." I do not mean maybe. I mean emphatically yes and emphatically no. That is to say, the answer

26

is "No" if one is looking for some kinds of uses and "Yes" if one is looking for other kinds of uses. Let us see how this comes about.

The first thing revealed by even a cursory but realistic acquaintance with the theory of games is that the theory provides no clues about how to play any specific game (except those invented for illustrative purposes). Thus, it is all very well to say that the game of diplomatic-military strategy is like a game of chess. Game theory teaches nothing about how to play chess, much less about how to play the diplomatic-military game, even if it were formulated as exactly as chess. It is all very well to say that business competition or an election campaign is like the game of poker. Game theory teaches nothing about playing poker (except an extremely simplified version of it, used for illustrative purposes only), much less how to compete successfully in business or how to be elected to office.

Game theory, in short, has nothing to do with gamesmanship or with "how to do it" recipes. I am afraid that the designation of game theory as a theory of rational conflict has given many people the impression (especially in the early days, when the theory was hailed as a great intellectual achievement) that the theory is a source of knowledge about how to conduct conflicts rationally. It is not.

What game theory does is to classify conflict situations in such a way that it becomes clear what the meaning of rationality is in each of the many different types of games. We have already seen that the meaning of rationality is different in contexts in which decisions must be made under conditions of risk (the outcomes being probabilistic) from what it is in the context in which decisions can be made under conditions of certainty. Game theory provides further classifications of decision situations.

For example, there is a fundamental distinction between two-person games and *N*-person games (with more than two players).

The distinction stems from the circumstance that if there are more than two players, some of them may form coalitions against others. The possibility of forming coalitions implies decision problems of a very different sort from those involved in two-person conflicts. Again, two-person games are subdivided into two categories—namely the zero-sum games and the non-zero-sum games. In the former, the algebraic sum of the winnings of the two "players" is always zero; i.e., whatever the outcome, the winnings of one are the losses of the other. In the latter, this is not necessarily the case. Again, the zero-sum games are subdivided into those with saddle points and those without saddle points. Associated with each choice of strategy by one of the players there is a "worst" outcome among all the possible outcomes of the choice. The best of this set of worst outcomes is called the minimax. If the outcome which is a minimax for one player is also a minimax for the other, the game is said to have a saddle point.

The meaning of "rational decision" involves different sorts of concepts in each of these cases and, as a matter of fact, becomes more and more nebulous as one progresses from the two-person zero-sum game with saddle points to the two-person zero-sum game without saddle points, to the two-person non-zero-sum game, to the *N*-person game. As the theory of autonomous rational decision becomes dissolved in ambiguities, other concepts must be brought in if the normative character of game theory (as implied by the term "rational decision") is to be preserved; one must bring in, for example, a concept of *equity* or of *arbitration principles* or of *social norms*. How and why these additional concepts must be introduced is, in my opinion, the principal heuristic result of game-theoretical analysis. The analysis provides *insights* into the nature of various types of conflict, not *answers* on how to conduct them, except possibly in the simplest cases of two-person zero-sum games.

Usually this discovery about the "impracticality" of game theory in real conflict situations is an occasion for disappointment with it. In the United States, in particular, the disappointment has instigated a "backlash" following initial enthusiasm for game theory. I have discussed these topics elsewhere at length and will only summarize my position in a few sentences. To the extent that one can derive from game theory ideas about the conduct of strategy in conflict situations (this can be done in some contexts to which the theory of the zero-sum game applies), the social value of game theory is open to misgivings. Presumably, the conflict situations that resemble zero-sum games most closely are cut-throat business competition and all-out war. Imparting strategic sophistication to participants in these conflicts seems to me a diversion of human talents and energies into primarily destructive channels. If such sophistication is achieved by one of the parties in such a struggle, this party achieves the power to inflict losses on rivals and so to accumulate excessive economic or political power. If, which is more likely, opponents in zero-sum struggles *both* increase their virtuosity in conducting such struggles, this leads only to an intensification of conflicts in human affairs.

Most human conflicts involve partially conflicting but partially coincident interests. Such conflicts, if they are represented by game models, must be represented by non-zero-sum games. However, game theory is not in a position to prescribe rational decisions definitively for non-zero-sum games (because of the ambivalence that creeps into the definition of rationality in these contexts). Here, I have argued, although game theory is not at fault, the pressure to cast situations in "researchable" terms

29

often leads strategists to "miscast" the situations as zero-sum games, a dangerous and often mischievous misconception. This is particularly true with respect to the tendency to see international political conflicts primarily in terms of military capabilities.

I should like, however, to dispel any impression I may have given by these arguments that because game theory has been misunderstood and misused it is for that reason useless or less than useless in social science, particularly in political theory. Along with the destructive criticism, I have also offered ways in which game theory could be put to constructive theoretical use—namely, as a source of insight into the nature of typically human conflict, in which the goals of decision-makers and their evaluations of other decision-makers' possible goals play the prominent part. In this way game theory is directly complementary to system theory, since the latter typically does not take these teleological and rationalistic (not to say "rational") components of conflict (and cooperation) into account.

HEURISTIC USES OF GAME THEORY

Here I shall confine myself to one or two examples. Consider the *N*-person game in so-called "characteristic function" form. In this formulation the total nature of the game—its rules, its players, the strategies open to them, etc.—is not considered; from the total complex are abstracted only the various combinations of players who can form coalitions. The game is defined if the amount to be won (in whatever units the pay-offs are made) is specified for each possible coalition that can form. That is, each coalition can guarantee itself a certain amount, and it is these guaranteed amounts that are specified.

Now in the original formulation of game theory it is shown that in all "interesting" situations of this sort a rational theory of decision is unable to specify which coalition should in fact form. No matter which coalition forms, there will be pressures operating to disrupt it. Therefore, if any kind of stability is to be expected in the coalition structure that obtains, extra-game theoretical considerations must be introduced, such as a "social inertia," which prevents too rapid realignment of coalitions, or "social norms," which prohibit some types of coalitions and encourage others. Here, then, is a theoretical result of great heuristic importance. It indicates *where to look* for factors that insure relative stability of existing coalitions wherever such coalitions occur.

Another by-product of *N*-person game theory is an extremely interesting mathematical theory of legislatures. It must be stressed at the outset that the mathematical theory of legislatures is in no way derived from observing how actual legislatures operate. It is based on a formal abstract model which assumes a legislature composed of a given number of members and a set of rules that indicate how a measure is to be passed. The theoretical results are no more and no less than a complete set of consequences *from these rules only*. The interest of the theory lies in the pursuit of these purely logical consequences, some of which are surprising and thought-provoking. Again this illustrates the purely heuristic value of the theory.

As a simple, almost trivial, example, consider a legislature composed of three members—A, B, and C—where A has two votes, and B and C have one vote each, but B has the privilege of breaking ties. We shall compare this with another legislature with members X, Y, and Z, in which each member has one vote. At first glance it seems that A and B are privileged vis-à-vis C, who has neither an extra vote nor the tie-breaking privilege; but, to see the actual situation, let us ask which are the "winning coalitions" in each of the legislatures—that is, which combinations can actually pass a measure. In the first legislature these are (A,B), (A,C), and (B,C) (the last being a winning coalition because B can break ties) and, of course, (A,B,C). The winning coalitions in the X, Y, Z legislature are exactly analogous. Thus the special voting arrangements in the first legislature have absolutely no influence on what it takes to pass a measure. It is this sort of analysis that constitutes the mathematical theory of legislatures.

The theory can deal with voting arrangements of arbitrary complexity, including multicameral systems, vetoes, overriding rules, etc., and can of course introduce additional assumptions about constraints on coalition formation. Incidentally, interest in this sort of mathematical theory goes back to Marquis de Condorcet in the eighteenth century.

As a by-product of such analysis, we have a formally precise definition of the *power* of a member of a formally defined legislature. The definition hinges on the notion of the "pivot"—i.e., the member who makes the deciding vote in a roll-call recording of votes, it being assumed that the order in which the roll is called is randomly selected. Of course, this definition of power is only a formal definition, not having necessarily to do with any actual power wielded by members of political blocs by virtue of their connections, their political virtuosity, their personalities, etc. However, calculation of the way this formally defined power is allotted among members of formally defined legislatures is an extremely thought-provoking exercise. For example, one of the results of such calculations is the discovery that about 98 per cent of the power residing in the United Nations Security Council is concentrated in the five permanent members. It has been calculated that an American president enjoys the greatest amount of power (so formally defined) when his party commands about a 55 per cent majority in Congress. (A greater majority makes the legislators of his own party more independent of him and so decreases his power.) It would be foolhardy to read immediate practical significance into these findings; but they do create a *framework of thought* in which future, more substantive theories relative to political science can be developed. Examples of such developments can be clearly seen in the work of William A. Gamson in sociology and William H. Riker in political science.

CONCLUDING REMARKS

I hope I have made clear what I mean when I speak of the heuristic value inherent in the model method. The dilemma in constructing social-scientific theories, particularly political theories, is the following. If one attempts to imitate the physical sciences—that is, to construct a predictive theory—one is of necessity confined to those aspects of social (in particular political) events that lend themselves to precise description, repeated observation, quantification, and other such objective treatment. Frequently this leads to trivialization of social theory. The reaction to such procedures is implied in the insistence in some quarters that the object of social science is not to predict or to control but to "understand." It is, of course, difficult to answer the question of what is meant by "understanding" if it is not predicated on the ability to predict. If objective evidence is lacking, "understanding" reduces to some sort of subjective satisfaction, an "inner glow," which, experience shows, can be seriously misleading. The true believers who subscribe to most dogmatic "systems" of philosophy, theology, or plain superstition can, with equal satisfaction, claim such inner "understanding." The model approach combines the rigor of hard science with the objectives of "soft science"—namely, the imparting of insight—for models can be perfectly rigorous in their construction and so

33

are connected to hard science through their origin. However, the goal of the models, as they are currently constructed in terms of system theory or in the framework of decision theory, is not prediction or control. The goal is heuristic: the imparting of understanding of the problems involved. In this way the model-oriented theory is connected with "soft science," the importance of which in the construction of political theory is not to be discounted.

In a way the social sciences find themselves in a position similar to that held by medicine a century ago and that held by psychiatry today. Before the discovery of the role of pathogenic microorganisms, the first major breakthrough in medicine, the science of healing can be said not to have existed at all, if one gauges a science by its practical achievements. If we look at medicine of a century ago through the jaundiced eye of a pragmatist, we have ample justification to dismiss it as quackery. The theories of disease promulgated in those days were preposterous, and the curative value of medical practice was probably not significantly greater than zero. What is said of mid-nineteenth-century medicine can also be said of present-day psychiatry and also of much of what goes today under the name of social science, including political theory. It would be wrong, however, to impugn proto-medical science on the grounds that it had no successes to point to. If we had not had the proto-medical science of yesterday, we certainly should not have the full-fledged medical science of today, for a science does not arise full-grown from a resolve to go about gathering knowledge "scientifically." A science develops in a certain climate, which includes a body of thinkers and practitioners of a proto-science whose ideas serve as raw material for the ideas of the science to be.

Finally, we should not discount the influence of the "theoretical climate" in political science on the framework within which decisions will be made. Consider the fundamental philosophical difference between the system-theoretical and the game-theoretical approach to political theory. The first, I have said, discounts the role of strategic decisions in political events and emphasizes the role of large-scale social and historical forces. System theory has, as we have noted, a deterministic flavor, the same flavor that appears in the historicism of Karl Marx and in the philosophies of history espoused by Tolstoy, Spengler, and Toynbee. It may be argued that this is by no means the whole truth about history in general or about political events in particular. Historical determinism is certainly not the whole truth; but it is part of the truth, perhaps a very important part.

System theory thus plays the part of a counterbalance to a political theory (of international politics) that loses itself in the labyrinths of ploys and counterploys that constitute life in the chancelleries. A connoisseur of diplomatic-military strategy and intrigue may shine in his analysis of all the factors that led to the decision by Austria to annex Bosnia and Herzegovina in 1908. To the system theorist this event is but a ripple in the tide that engulfed Europe at the turn of the century. From the system-theoretical point of view, it was the structure of the system and the interactions within it that led to war directly and inexorably. If this view is correct, then the machinations in the chancelleries may have had no more historical significance than the long-forgotten, mixed-up genealogies of European monarchical dynasties, which once served as the framework of international politics. To the system theorist, war is a form of behavior characteristic of the system of national states. The intricate "causes" of specific wars, of interest to the historian or the political theorist, are of little interest to the system theorist concerned with the gross outlines of international behavior or with the grosser outlines of human history. I do not think that this point of view is to be discounted, lest we lose sight of the forest for the trees.

On the other hand, Richardson himself said that his equations represent only what would happen if people did not stop to think. The rational, or at least the calculating, component of political behavior is certainly not to be ignored just because it tends to disappear in the large outline of history.

Thus system-theoretical and rational-decision approaches to political theory complement each other. Each emphasizes what the other largely ignores. Acquaintance with both approaches ought to have an effect on the intellectual climate in which political theory is pursued; and if this climate has any effect at all on political decisions (and I am convinced that it does even in the most antitheoretically oriented modus operandi such as ours), then theory has its uses in the study of politics. That is, theory, via its effect on students of political affairs, who in turn have some effect on the political climate in which political decisions are made, does, even though possibly very indirectly, influence political decisions. We can hope, therefore, that as theory becomes more sophisticated and self-critical, so will the political decisions.

The Making of Foreign Policy in the United States

CHARLES BURTON MARSHALL

In discussing policy-making at the center of authority in our system, I propose to focus on foreign policy as the aspect of public affairs most familiar to me. Even as thus scaled down, the topic is still a huge one. Particular foreign policies may relate to particular situations abroad and involve particular aspects of relations among organized societies—scientific, technological, economic, commercial, cultural, legal, humanitarian, ideological, military, diplomatic, and so on through many categories. Particular foreign policies may be of passing or of enduring import. Foreign policy, as a category comprising the government's efforts to affect events and conditions in the world beyond its jurisdiction favorably to our national preferences as understood by those in authority, extends over the great globe itself, transcends all categories of relationship, and fuses the immediate with remote futurity.

Should I deal with the making of policy in this field as the procedure of decision; as the calculation of interplay among United States intentions and those of hostile, friendly, and indifferent entities and forces in world affairs; or as the philosophic problem of selecting among values and means in trying to make headway in an obdurate environment? Pondering that question calls up a number of pertinent reminiscences.

Several years ago I was asked by the Sunday magazine section of a great metropolitan newspaper to write a piece giving a formula for making foreign policy. I declined. In my view, ways of making foreign policy were as numerous as ways of annoying one's wife, and an attempt to subsume them into one sovereign pattern could only issue in something misleadingly formal with small relevance to events. The proponent was as impatient with my skepticism as I was with the whole idea, and the resulting argument clarified his motivating preconception. To his mind, foreign policy was a cumulative process like a river. At its inception a policy would trickle forth from some identifiable spring, whence it would follow a definable channel of development. Along the way various offices and agencies of government in verifiable order would debouch their wisdom like tributaries. Finally, at some weary distance from the source, the policy would wind safely to the sea of history as an achieved reality. I was assumed to be familiar with this river's somewhat mysterious valley and qualified to map it—like Lewis and Clark feeling their way along and revealing the course of the Columbia—and perhaps to recommend ways to speed the flow by straightening and dredging the channel here and there.

I could not do so, and cannot now, but my second recollection is of someone's attempt at the formulation I declined to try. This person happens to be an addict of model-building, a diagramer of concepts with one of the burgeoning institutions devoted to research pertaining to external affairs. I digress to observe the proliferation of such institutions during recent years. At a meeting within the government a while back—I happened to be present—

38

someone suggested a need for developing a catalogue of such institutions and their projects. Someone else affirmed that a number of such catalogues already existed. A proposal was then entered for making a catalogue of the catalogues.

When the man who had diagramed policy-making showed me the product of his cerebrations, a marvel of labyrinthine intricacy consisting of vertical and horizontal lines arrow-pointed and transfixing a series of circles of varying diameter, I had an impression of having seen it before. Then I remembered. It was a reasonable facsimile of the wiring plan of my stereo phonograph, even to the detail of several terminal speakers, the central and largest of them labeled "President."

Yet a third memory concerns what is known as a summer study—a process in vogue with some of the more affluent units of the bureaucracy. The idea is to gather, and to hold together under conditions of close interchange for six or seven weeks at some sequestered place, an array of reputedly learned outsiders for the purpose of pondering some sector of policy. The product is supposed to be fresh thinking. The process works. The thinking done at the one I was involved in three summers ago was indeed fresh. Eminent scientists were among the participants—some of them as roving and self-assured and exhilaratingly free of the trammels of scientific rigor as perhaps only a scientist parted from his specialty can be. In session after session, one experienced the grand pleasures of dealing with a rational, wholly calculable, and plastic world, with established norms and pervading uniformities. One obdurate situation after another was sorted out into A's, B's, and C's linked with numerical coefficients, allocated to numerator and denominator, and equated with a solution. Thus a legitimate order was arranged for Africa; Arabs and Israelis and Indians and Pakistanis were reconciled; China was soothed and converted; the Soviet Union was rendered amenable to inspection; a world police force was recruited, trained, and deployed; and mankind was at last brought to teleological unity— all on blackboards.

A contrasting memory remains from a so-called war game I engaged in two years ago. For those of you not familiar with such activity, a war game is not war but a game—an elegant and protracted kind of charade, with refined rules and meticulous umpiring. Characteristically, a hypothetical incident is blown into a crisis and carried through to a denouement. The participants are divided into interacting groups of decision-makers, walled off from one another and communicating their hypothetical actions and responses through a central control agency, which fogs up the information to simulate real life before distributing it. The exercise is enjoyable and educative, resembling reality much as the game of monopoly resembles operating in the market—with gains and losses that excite without enriching and pain without hurting. On the occasion in question I was one-fifth of a United States notional government. An admired and scholarly friend was the simulated President. We were pitted against wily and determined adversaries in a putative confrontation growing out of an infiltration scrape involving a far country. We smote them hip and thigh and came off with a considerable diplomatic success. I wish the nation might always do as well in real situations.

My friend the President for a week-end was deeply impressed by the simulated experience of having to make decisions in face of incomplete and refracted information, being stuck with one's decisions as irrevocable facts, and finding one's estimates of probabilities continuously overtaken and upset in part in consequence of the very actions taken in pursuance of one's estimate of probabilities. The postulated situation was continuously becoming unraveled. Decisions never quite worked out to match intentions. The game had brought home to him a discomforting appreciation of a lesson, as expressed by James Gould Cozzens, that "the Nature of Things abhors a drawn line and loves a hodgepodge, resists consistency and despises drama."[1] He was concerned, too, over how, in acting the role, he had found himself constrained to conform to the premises and modes of thought and expression he had criticized when they were manifested by those filling such a role in reality, and how, much as he wished to focus decisions away from the exigent present and to orient them to some loftier and more enduring conception of purpose, he had found himself pressed inexorably to deal with the perverse problem at hand.

My last pertinent recollection is the only one drawn from experience in government. In a late phase of the Truman administration, someone in the councils of policy thought up a scheme for instituting a psychological-strategy board. It would function at what is called the White House level. It was hoped that the board would be a source of imagination and a spur to diligence in the handling of external affairs. It would bend every effort. It would invent ways to seize the initiative. These purposes were arrived at without critical regard for limiting circumstances. The field at any moment is all too likely to be strewn with bent efforts. There is always an array of initiatives conceivably to be seized, and some of them are the last things any regime in its right mind would wish to lay hold of. *The* initiative is an abstraction quite different from an aggregate of particular initiatives. In any event, the aim was to inject a dynamic quality into the conduct of foreign policy. Dynamism—a concept borrowed from mechanics or physics—figures in many a cliché about the proper handling of external affairs. I do not know what meaning it has beyond describing a tendency of processes to take over on their own and to produce effects not intended by the originator. This sort of thing

41

happens in foreign policy; but, although inevitable, it is not good. Anyway, the thing to do under the romance of the moment was to make everything dynamic.

Some of us in the State Department were leary of the venture, but the Under Secretary of the time, in the determining role, regarded the project as a bureaucratic inevitability to be accepted and then contained. That last turned out to be an unrealistic expectation. Assemble a sizable cadre of bureaucrats with a warrant for activity and a record of accomplishment to make in order to justify existence and a suite of offices and some telephones, and the result is inherently uncontainable. I am not going to recount what came of the project. My remembrance is confined to a brief experience as an interim member of an interdepartmental group set up to guide it. At our first meeting the new staff supplied each of us with something called a planning kit. It contained a ball-point pen, a set of color pencils, a protractor, a writing pad, a list of governments with names of their chiefs and the parties in power, and a world map done in the Mercator projection, with the earth's surface rolled out from a center in Europe and the perimeters sheered off at distended poles and in the mid-Pacific.

Each of the recollections recounted is of some help. The initiative conceived as faddish activism or as tactical audacity is delusory. The initiative as a concept of having power enough to make choices is vital. Fliers speak of a function called the power curve —a notional arc indicating the margins available to a pilot in various phases of flight. At the apex the plane has full momentum with minimal expenditure of resources—plus a high reserve of fuel. On the inclining slope the motors are pressed to get under way and to attain conditions of equilibrium with a heavy load. On the declining slope, momentum is diminishing despite expenditure of ebbing resources. To buck either slope is to be behind the power curve. There mischance is more likely to occur simply because the pilot is less able to cope with it. In policy—to apply an imperfect metaphor—woe comes in being caught behind the power curve.

In policy, as in aviation, the choice of destinations is not the hard part. The test of the art comes in nurturing the momentum and the margins to permit one to move on to them. I would not disparage altogether the relevance or the value of goals as expressions of world conditions as we should like to see them if granted power to actualize our wishes. The aspect of foreign policy concerned with formulating preferences for the long run is quite simple and easy. The long run, however, can in fact be only an aggregate of short runs; and the demands imposed in an endless succession of short runs rise from reaches of the world beyond our fiat and inclined to be recalcitrant to our preferences. Forward planning is necessary, not because the future is predictable, but because it is not. Its aim is not to foreclose choice in the future but to preserve the possibility of choice. It does not involve the drawing-up of formulas far in advance of events to be dealt with, but it requires unremitting attention to the deferred consequences of instant decisions. Foreign policy always takes form in the exigent present. In that sense, the war game was valid, but the summer study was of small value.

Anyone dealing responsibly with the equations of foreign policy must bring to bear some image of the world. It may be an image as distorted and misinforming as the Mercator projection. Indeed, it is virtually bound to be an imperfect image, highly conditioned by subjective elements, because it is, I venture, beyond any of us to encompass the planet whole in his mind's eye. Any perspective is inherently arbitrary in being projected from some particular set of coordinates, and the earth's multifariousness defies any individual's momentary perception. Dealing with foreign policy

43

requires also some sense of history. By that phrase I do not mean merely a grasp of chronology of recorded events. I mean some set of assumptions as to what counts in broad affairs; what are the leverages of effectiveness; and what are the relations between reality and will, will and action, and action and reality. Such a sense of history may be loaded with romance and futile hopes. It may be clued to forbearance and caution. Whether reflective of reason or of delusion, some sense of history prevails in every choice made in the field of foreign policy. No one of us can escape history, in the sense that we are conditioned by some set of norms, wishes, and expectations as precepts derived from the past and projected into the future.

These considerations have a bearing on presidential primacy in foreign policy. I do not mean to affirm, as a pedantic absolute, that the President makes foreign policy. That function involves a complex of institutions. Nevertheless, the President's major significance in the wiring plan is obvious and needs no labored diagraming. His constitutional roles as chief executive, as commander-in-chief, as proponent of legislation, as wielder of the appointment prerogative, as custodian of the recognition power, and as chief agent in international negotiations are enhanced under contemporary conditions. Great sums are dispensed at his discretion. He carries the weight of the man who could press the button. He bears authority derived from the fact and the reputation of having unequaled access to privileged information—a huge factor of power. The communication media are at his disposal when he wants them, and what he says echoes at once over the world. He epitomizes the nation abroad, and he is in position to be its pre-eminent preceptor at home. These institutional attributes apply to any President. My concern here, however, is not the institutional constants but individual differentiations.

With a President, as with any of us, his grasp of the world and his measure of the unfolding future is a projection of himself and of the past as he is given to understand it. For a President, these matters are of historic moment, whereas for any of us they are personal details only. A President's constitutional and institutional positions are patent, but one is left to construe as best one can the operative assumptions in a President's mind. Presidents have been variant in the accessibility of their relevant ideas. Some have been inclined to wear their philosophies on their sleeves. Others have been more guarded. Some—Woodrow Wilson, for instance—have taken care to make their important discourses their very own. Others—I forbear to name names—have relied on a galaxy of writers, leaving an observer to wonder about the real authorship of their memorable utterances.

As a matter of custom, Presidents are wont to profess humility on occasion; but they are as a class susceptible to the sorts of vanity that beset us all. Indeed, an extra portion thereof may have been required for impulsion toward the apex of authority. The circumstances prevailing there—especially so in contemporary times—are such as to puff them up and to draw them toward that heroic view of history handed down from epochs when great events were recorded as episodes in the biographies of monarchs. Their approval is importuned by an endless round of visitors. Every available presidential utterance, even if commonplace, is assured public attention. Their personalities, habits, and tastes— and by extension those of their families as well—are reported and remarked upon as of general significance. They are gazed at and cheered by multitudes. Presidents bear the consciousness of being vested with fateful and prodigious powers. Their counselors and aides, although not necessarily sycophants, are anxious for good standing. The impediments to critical advice are formidable, for even the most candid and courageous of subordinates are likely to be affected by the aura surrounding their chiefs. The wonder is not that Presidents are tempted toward the heroic view but that some of them manage not to succumb to it.

The heroic view encourages a President to regard the conduct of foreign relations as a clubby sort of business shared in by himself and his counterparts in other major lands. He sees himself cast as a great mover and shaker. The courses of history are reverberations of moving and shaking done at summits of authority. He may be indifferent to history conceived as the sum total of the lessons of human experience, such as they are, antecedent to the instant situation, and he may be preoccupied instead with that finite aspect of history marking his association with its processes. The world takes on a high degree of plasticity. This view encourages him to put a premium on his own cluster of impressions of the exterior world as the most authentic image of reality, one worthy of sovereign credence. Such a President, commonly said to be his own Secretary of State, inclines to counsel generated by his own entourage in preference to any other—this because it carries his brand. He probably prefers his own confidants as emissaries for critical missions. He may unconsciously ascribe to himself inherent virtues of personality—akin to the healing potential anciently believed to be an attribute of kings—and so set great store on face-to-face encounters with his counterparts abroad.

At an opposed extreme, a President may recognize his ascendancy in decision-making as only a transient circumstance—and may be aware that the same is true for his counterparts in other regimes. Most of the problems he and they must deal with probably have originated long before their advent to authority; and all too many of the problems will have to be passed along to their successors, altered perhaps but not solved. The world situation does not have the plasticity implicit in the heroic view. It is obdurate. History is not the handiwork of Presidents and potentates. It is the life of nations. The wisdom for getting along in it is never, by far, all in one man's head. A good portion of it is stored in institutions that antedated his arrival in office and will be there after his departure.

It would be oversimple to link Presidents categorically with one view or the other. They may combine them, and they may vary the combination from one phase to another in relation to their experience with the vicissitudes of office and perhaps in relation to their sense of the nation's position along the power curve at any particular juncture. Insight into the limitations of choice in policy appears to be a recurring lesson gained from deepened familiarity with presidential power, and its effects are variable.

An appropriate time span over which to attempt a comparison of successive Presidents in this regard is the interval since the onset of the second disintegration in our century of a Europe-centered order—roughly the last thirty-five years. Mr. Hoover's presidency was the one overtaken by that baffling development; hence one can only speculate on the quality of his conduct of great authority under favorable conditions. Mr. Hoover's natural inclination was to proceed "in the belief that by application of logical systems, by deductions from the measurable, statistically accountable data, the important matters in life could be held in place," Elting Morison observes in an eminent biography of the Secretary of State of that time, Henry L. Stimson.[2] A President with such preconceptions recoiled from the sullen and disturbed world environment of the early 1930's. On one notable occasion, his Secretary of State lectured him on political leadership in face of imponderables:

> Human affairs, he said, were "not like building a bridge"—
> not every stress could be projected and calculated; "in the move-
> ment of great currents of human opinions . . . you could make

47

your plans only for a certain distance. . . ." Any effort "to foresee it all" led to an appearance of timidity and vacillation. From the law and the army, he went on, he had found that "In case of doubt . . . march toward the guns."[3]

As adversity wore on, Mr. Morison recounts, the travail of Europe became "secondary for America . . . to the travail of the United States and of the President himself."[4] He found himself increasingly at odds with a Secretary in whose view "Righteousness should be as bold as lions against the adversary." As the "world of Herbert Hoover and Henry Stimson came tumbling down," Mr. Morison observes, "the strain placed on the carefully arranged relations between the two men was greatly increased. Often enough they found themselves working not so much in a crossness of purpose as of spirit, in that uneasiness produced by the feeling of not being understood."[5] Those broad measures on which they found limited concord—the debt moratorium, disarmament, adherence to the World Court, and the attempt to offer the United States' oblique support to the fragile hope of general action to counter aggression—were barren of substantial results. Through it all, Mr. Hoover wore his authority as a hair shirt. The initiative in foreign policy lay with his Secretary, with Mr. Hoover as the nay-sayer.

Mr. Roosevelt wore his prerogatives like a plumed hat—but only in the last half of his twelve years in the White House. Preoccupied with domestic affairs, in the first phase he left external concerns mostly to Secretary Hull. A Roosevelt speech of 1936 stands as a supreme expression of the isolationist sentiment then rife. The President acquiesced in Congress' ill-conceived design in the successive Neutrality Acts to predetermine foreign policy in event of hostilities abroad and implicitly to hedge in the executive power. The first attempt at a reversal of course, in the so-called Quarantine Speech at Chicago in 1937, was ambiguous and tepid. The subsequent overtures to head off renewal of general hostilities lacked focus. Nothing in the early record adumbrated his conduct after the lapse of Europe's twenty-year armistice. Thenceforth Mr. Roosevelt was in personal—very personal —command of United States foreign policy and was the nation's constant, if sometimes artful, preceptor.

Some of the lines of action stemmed from grants of authority enacted by Congress and broadly interpreted—for example, the destroyer-base deal, the lend-lease program, the progressively tighter embargo on Japan. Others were exercises of inherent executive discretion—the step-by-step entry into undeclared maritime war with Germany in the Atlantic, the deployment to Iceland, and the collaboration with the United Kingdom in defining war aims, capped by that notable episode at Argenta when the conditions for a transformed world order were uttered in a press release. The turn from quasi-war to war intensified the course. Here we cannot labor the details of the Washington and Quebec meetings, Casablanca, Tehran, Cairo, and Yalta; but there the heroic view of policy-making was portrayed as never before or since in our history. Much of what was done proved illusory or evanescent. Some of it has worked out ironically—the aim of great-power status for China and giving the back of the hand to Charles de Gaulle, for instance. Mr. Roosevelt was using his prerogatives to the limit both as negotiator and as commander-in-chief. He put a premium on personal emissaries and on the efficacy of personal presence. The illusion of summitsmanship—great men of history in concert ordaining the future— was at the full.

It is easy to misjudge the policy undertakings incident to the war years—too easy to write them down as exercises in improvidence and to hypothesize greatly different outcomes, all to the advantage of our interests, given only an additional portion of sophistication and resolution and less anxiety for accommodation with Josef Stalin. The great margins in means available in the closing phases of hostilities and after the enemy collapse had not been at hand throughout the struggle. It is pointless to criticize the Roosevelt wartime policies as if the United States had been at the apex of the power curve all along. In fair appraisal, however, style did exceed substance. Mr. Roosevelt's great utterances, read now, seem to stir rather than to instruct. There is much in them about fashioning the future, but little to lend understanding of the present. Clearly, also, he took too readily at face value the apparent concord, under the pressures of a shared belligerency, among the triumvirs of Tehran and Yalta, counted too heavily on hope of institutionalizing the wartime coalition as the basis for an enduring system of order and security, and in deference to that hope fobbed off too many important matters as secondary. It is hard for statesmen to acknowledge misconceptions, to swallow words, and to alter vaunted courses. Mr. Roosevelt was spared the necessity. The task fell to another.

On the morning after his sudden advent to the presidency Mr. Truman instructed some of his staff to draft for him an address to the people and suggested they get collaboration from Dean Acheson, remembered as a helpful Assistant Secretary of State handling congressional relations when Mr. Truman was a senator in charge of a committee trying to spur the war effort. Summoned to the White House, Mr. Acheson found the staff men searching Roosevelt speeches for appropriate quotations. What counted now was not what a deceased President had said but what the living President had on his mind, Mr. Acheson insisted. He knocked on the President's door, found him in lone contemplation, and put the query to him. Mr. Truman was abashed by the idea of attaching central significance to his thoughts but was pressed into voicing them while notes were taken. A while later a draft was ready. Mr. Truman exclaimed in amazement on finding it an expression of his own ideas; wondered aloud that they should be found worth communicating; and was told that on this point no other person's judgment should be interposed, since Mr. Truman was now the President.

Fortunately, Mr. Truman, as Vice President, had not been in the inner circle of policy. He had to go through a difficult period of initiation as President, but there was no mortgage on his spirit and reputation. On balance, his newness was an asset. Precipitated into supreme responsibility, Mr. Truman found awesome the dimension of the huge and multifarious world he had to deal with and the large purposes he was called upon to shoulder. He seems to have had some doubts about measuring up to the requirements of the heroic concept of policy-making. Within two years he had learned that the ranges of time and space involved in foreign policy, however huge, must yet be broken down into tactically manageable portions—something to handle from one exigency to another. It was not so awesome a world after all. Mr. Truman came to see it, himself, and the making of foreign policy in proper proportion. Potsdam disenthralled him on summitry. He set value in institutions more than in personality. He neither abdicated to the bureaucracy nor lorded over it. He familiarized himself with problems without dissipating time and energies on operational minutiae. His anger was hot and brief, not sullen and lingering. Men as willful, proud, and resourceful as Mr. Acheson and George Marshall never presumed against his ascendancy. He rated well as a decision-maker, notwithstanding that he was hustled by bad advice into an improvident closure of lend-lease—a cardinal error, which resulted in a two-year hiatus in effectively aiding postwar recovery—and that he was too patient far too long on the MacArthur question. Some of his off-the-cuff public discourse on policy was ill-considered. Some of his diplomatic appointments were anomalous—a phenomenon not peculiar to him. Yet he did well. Never prone to see himself as a great mover and shaker, Mr. Truman nevertheless made a record of considerable accomplishment.

The United States was singular in having emerged from World War II with its capital plant more productive than at the beginning. It had been spared invasion, occupation, and bombardment. Its public life was intact. It was the world's great source of credit and supplies, and it had a transient monopoly in nuclear capability. The relative position, in sum, was favorable. At the same time a hard lesson about the finiteness of even great power was being rubbed in on the Americans, especially in regard to China. For the Truman administration it was a case, then, of fair headway in a stormy passage. The Eisenhower administration succeeded it on a proposition of resuming some lost efficacy of spirit and action in world affairs—a theme pervasive in the victorious campaign of 1952. President Eisenhower deputed the task to his Secretary of State, John Foster Dulles, with a completeness of delegation usually associated with military command. Through six years of unprecedented personal activity, the Secretary enacted a heroic concept of policy-making—but at a ministerial level. Under deferential supervision Mr. Dulles ran foreign policy. The summit episodes, with Mr. Eisenhower in the central role, and the President's ventures in personal diplomacy in the grand tours undertaken near the end of his tenure, after Mr. Dulles had gone, were at best imposing rather than important. In appraising the conduct of foreign affairs one must always try to distinguish between things doing and things done—between goals proclaimed and aims achieved and between activism and action—and this pertains to the Eisenhower administration.

In a late phase, the President himself spoke knowledgeably of the baffling obduracy of world affairs in answer to a reporter's question:

> I think that general policy is good. But in all sorts of, in every single situation that comes up, you have got a new problem and here is one of your troubles today. There is no single, there is no possibility in any single instance that I know of where you can isolate a problem between the country you represent, say, and the one I represent. You try to do something and it affects three other countries, and I don't care where you go, whether you go to the Mideast, you go to the Far East, if you talk to Formosa, you are affecting someone else. If you are talking France, you are talking about somebody else, and it is the same way, whether it's Tunisia or anything else. So that the carrying on of foreign policy is a very intricate business, and it becomes a, you might say, almost an art rather than any science, and I believe that free countries such as ours have got to observe the principles that we observe among ourselves: live and let live.

Pressed by another question, the President continued:

> That is a very complicated thing, and so far as I know—and I have sat in many of these conferences—the individuals that come to see us state exactly what I am stating to you now. That is so complicated that you have to go—you try to lay out a program, a plan, but it—work it if you have got it here, if you go here you have to defend from that, you have to move over here.
>
> It is a very difficult, intricate thing, and I don't care what head of state or government has been here or that I have gone to see has acknowledged the intricacies of today in manipulating what you might say the foreign plans of any free country.[6]

A different expression of the same idea came from Mr. Eisenhower's successor after two years of his tragically shortened presidency. At the threshold Mr. Kennedy put emphasis on style—civility, as he called it in the inaugural. His approach to foreign policy was much in the manner of Franklin D. Roosevelt's second phase—"a personalized pattern with . . . stress on open options and close control," in Richard E. Neustadt's phrase.[7] He dipped deeply into operational matters. His press conferences displayed dazzlingly his grasp of empirical details—not necessarily evidence, however, of wise allocation of time and energies. The White House staff, as the immediate instrumentality of a President devoted to being his own Secretary of State, became a sort of second—if not first—Department of State. Mr. Kennedy relied heavily on personal legates. His resort to direct, confidential correspondence with counterparts in other regimes was unprecedented in frequency and diversity—however questionable its utility. He often went abroad himself on missions, with results more dramatic than productive. The Vienna tête-à-tête might better have never occurred. The visit to President de Gaulle surely did not help. The ironic potential of presidential diplomacy was perhaps most clearly shown in an assemblage with Central American Presidents, who joined ours in an eloquent avowal on behalf of constitutional processes, whereafter several of them were soon bowled over by unconstitutional processes.

President Kennedy answered with the voice of experience when asked the lessons of two years in office:

> Well, I think in the first place the problems are more difficult than I had imagined they were. Secondly, there is a limitation upon the ability of the United States to solve these problems. We are involved now in the Congo in a very difficult situation. We have been unable to secure an implementation of the policy which we have supported. We are involved in a good many other areas. We are trying to see if a solution can be found to the struggle between Pakistan and India, with whom we want to maintain friendly relations. Yet they are unable to come to an agreement. There is a limitation, in other words, upon the power of the United States to bring about solutions.

I think our people get awfully impatient and maybe fatigued and tired, and saying "We have been carrying this burden for 17 years; can we lay it down?" We can't lay it down, and I don't see how we are going to lay it down in this century.

So that I would say that the problems are more difficult than I had imagined them to be. The responsibilities placed on the United States are greater than I imagined them to be, and there are greater limitations upon our ability to bring about a favorable result than I had imagined them to be. And I think that is probably true of anyone who becomes President, because there is such a difference between those who advise or speak or legislate, and between the man who must select from the various alternatives proposed and say that this shall be the policy of the United States. It is much easier to make the speeches than it is to finally make the judgments. . . .[8]

Mr. Kennedy's most highly reputed success came in the handling of the missile crisis, through improvisation in face of an unforeseen event; and none of his large plans can be said yet to have come to fulfillment—another index to the adventitiousness of foreign policy. The record, however, of that administration—taken as literature—is abundant. Surely no other President ever articulated so well, so persistently, about foreign affairs. Therewith I come to a doubt. Did he or his writers articulate too well?

He said graceful things about fostering diversity over the globe —as if there would not be enough without our cultivation. He often repeated an apothegm—as compact as an Alexander Pope couplet—about never negotiating from fear and never fearing to negotiate. It remains a puzzler. What would spur governments to negotiate on security matters except fear of consequences of not agreeing? A third illustrative instance of the late President's articulateness is his statement that "our Nation is commissioned by history to be either an observer of freedom's failure or the cause of its success." I defer to Dr. Henry Wriston's description of those words as paling de Gaulle's concept of *grandeur* and equaling Khrushchev's most comprehensive claims on the future. "It would be difficult to find a more felicitous sentence or a more sweeping declaration of our presumed power to shape the destiny of mankind," he goes on. In Dr. Wriston's appraisal,

> That scintillant sentence raises profound questions whether we really believe in "self-determination," if I may cite one of Wilson's dangerous phrases. . . .Cold analysis, in a word, makes it obvious that by ourselves we cannot "cause" the success of freedom. In making that assertion, however, the President was giving voice to what a great many members of Congress, and of the American public, believe in their sub-conscious minds. The American messianic temper still survives.[9]

Professor Neustadt—equipped by inside knowledge immeasurably better than I to evaluate the late President as actor, as distinguished from preceptor, in this field—has depicted Mr. Kennedy as having "apparently absorbed in his short time a lesson Franklin Roosevelt never learned about the Russians . . .: that in another country an *effective* politician can have motives very *different* from his own." The observation is followed by an exclamation: "What an advantageous lesson to have learned in two years' time!" I should have thought the point to be purely elementary and am puzzled that it was not assumed as a datum from the outset. The difference lights up the difficulties of judgment. In Professor Neustadt's summation, the late President as head of the policy process had gone "quite a way toward mastery in two years and ten months." He adds, "We shall not know how far he might have got."[10]

Great assurances of change customarily accompany a transfer of the presidency because of expiration of a mandate, and a beholder is thereafter impressed by the degree of continuity. High assurances of continuity mark any succession due to a President's death, and then change sets in. Thus it has been so in the shift from a Kennedy to a Johnson administration. President Johnson differs from his predecessor in style at least—and style has something to do with substance. He shows less urgency about the operational and empirical details of policy. My impression is that, in comparison to his predecessor, he is more interested in prevailing, is more inclined to address any problem by first asking what we want to do about it, and is less prone to believe that the answers to great issues can be arrived at by churning through the data.

The emphasis on the presidential staff as distinguished from the executive departments has subsided. The relation to the State Department in particular has changed. President Johnson, in contrast to the late President Kennedy, is inclined to govern through the department rather than around it or even against it. Changes in style bordering on changes in substance have occurred. It would be hard to imagine a Kennedy administration, solicitous as it was of the neophyte states, declining official reception to an inter-African delegation sent over to remonstrate and to consult about the new turn in United States policy on the Congo. Presumably our policy regarding that country will henceforth be run with a view to trying to help manage its problems rather than with a view to trying to cultivate approval and favor among its neighbors—a salutary change. Similar modifications in other aspects of our foreign policy may add up to a considerable shift from the practices of Mr. Johnson's predecessor.

Great tests of the President's mettle must surely lie ahead. We can dismiss as entirely improbable the expectation, which one repeatedly hears or reads about in the wake of the election, to the effect that foreign policy will be a less prominent and pressing concern as the President moves from an inherited to an elected tenure and takes up a mandate of his own. That happy situation is surely not in the cards. Disintegrative forces are at work in the

Atlantic alliance. Latin America presents a great potential for trouble. Too long, perhaps because of reluctance to face up to hard requirements with an election campaign on, the situation in Vietnam has been permitted to deteriorate, with dire implications for the rest of Southeast Asia. Red China will surely be a more active and menacing force in times ahead. The Indian subcontinent is riven with bitter issues which cannot be counted on to remain dormant. The same should be said for the problems of the Middle East. The notion that the exterior world is going to provide us respite from foreign policy issues is as baseless an idea as I can imagine.

We shall be able to judge Mr. Johnson as a leader in foreign policy more fully when, despite his preferences, he has to deal with a great array of exigencies that will soon be crowding in on his attention. The campaign afforded few clues. The level of discourse was disappointing. In James Reston's phrase, "the nation . . . lost something."[11] It lost an opportunity for a cogent debate about foreign policy. The challenger did not exact much, and so little was vouchsafed in response. I did note, however, one presidential pronouncement which, at face value, would foreclose the United States from ever issuing an ultimatum.[12] The idea is appropriate as a wish but not as a pledge. No one can be sure that this government will henceforth be freed of necessity of giving peremptory warning to an adversary. Each of us must wish our President well at the threshold of a term of his own. May he be spared occasion to renounce the cited pronouncement. In event of a dire requirement, may he have the wisdom to abandon that gratuitous self-restriction. May he be saved from temptations of expecting too much, of placing undue hopes in the transfiguring power of personality, and of overdoing the rhetoric. May he govern—and may he be judged—in accord with propositions and insights that I describe by quoting from a wise Englishman:

58

One cause of error is to assume that statesmen have a free hand to do as they will, when in truth they so often have to act in compelling situations which they have inherited and under pressure of circumstances which they cannot control. . . .

A second error is, as Sir Llewellyn Woodward once said, to attribute to actors on the stage of history a capacity to pierce the future which men do not possess, and to condemn them if they do not shape their courses accordingly. "We, who do not know tomorrow, assume that men of yesterday knew today and that every sower can foresee every harvest."

Finally it is well to recognize the limits of human endeavor; to realize that the business of government is not an academic exercise; to reconcile oneself to the fact that there are no neat and final solutions, that international affairs are a fabric without much of a pattern, and that diplomacy is most often, as von Moltke said of strategy, a succession of expedients; to suspect that bold initiatives, imaginative gestures, stirring leads and elaborate blueprints of policy, so beloved of those who are free of responsibilities of government, are seldom of the stuff of practical statesmanship in international relations. . . .[13]

NOTES

1. James Gould Cozzens, *Guard of Honor* (London: Longmans, Green, 1949), p. 572.

2. Elting Morison, *Turmoil and Tradition* (Boston: Houghton Mifflin, 1960), p. 305.

3. *Ibid.,* p. 313.

4. *Ibid.,* p. 404.

5. *Ibid.,* p. 415.

6. *New York Times,* May 29, 1958.

7. Richard E. Neustadt, "Kennedy in the Presidency: A Premature Appraisal," *Political Science Quarterly,* September, 1964, p. 327.

8. *Washington Post and Times-Herald,* December 16, 1962.

9. *Address by Henry M. Wriston on the Occasion of His Election as Honorary President of the Council on Foreign Relations, April 6, 1964* (Stamford, Conn.: The Overbrook Press, 1964), p. 11.

10. Neustadt, p. 328.

11. *New York Times,* October 30, 1964.

12. *Ibid.,* September 26, 1964.

13. Lord William Strang, *Britain in World Affairs* (New York: Praeger, 1961), pp. 18-19.

Approaches to the Understanding of International Politics

QUINCY WRIGHT

A knowledge of international politics is important for national decision-makers, for their professional advisors and agents, for research workers in the field, and for the average citizen. The latter has to make up his mind on the broad objectives of foreign policy in order to contribute to public opinion, which necessarily guides the maker of foreign policy, especially in democracies. In other forms of government public opinion cannot be ignored, although doubtless dictatorships have a greater capacity to influence it through their control of the instruments of mass communication. The citizen in a democracy also has to make up his mind at election time on the personality who he thinks will best implement these broad objectives. Foreign policy has increasingly taken precedence over domestic policy in national elections. Before the 1964 presidential election the pollsters found that foreign-policy issues involving war and peace and the control of nuclear weapons were regarded as of major importance by more than a third of those interviewed. A smaller proportion gave priority to the quasi-international issue of civil rights; and much smaller proportions, to such domestic issues as federal-state relations, federal taxes, social legislation, and freedom of economic enterprise.

The approach of the decision-maker is likely to be the same as that of average citizens, because he usually comes from them and, in a democracy, is elected because he shares their views. Doubtless, when making decisions he should know much more about international politics than does the average citizen; but he will have to get this knowledge from his professional advisors, although his experience in both domestic and international politics will be helpful. Michael Polanyi has distinguished "personal knowledge" gained from experience from "scientific knowledge" gained from books, and believes that the former is much more important than the latter in the practice of an art, especially the art of politics. The practical decision-maker, who must believe in a voluntaristic universe in which his decision will make a difference, necessarily has a different orientation from the scientist, who seeks predictive formulas and who must believe that the universe is at least partly determined, tying the future to the past in some measure.

The average citizen may not have had much experience in political decision-making, but he must believe that the decisions that he makes in casting a ballot or voicing an opinion are important and will have an effect on the future course of events.

The citizen and the decision-maker, therefore, differ from the professional advisor, who presumably has a great deal of scientific knowledge useful to predict the probable course of events and the probable consequences of alternative decisions, but usually in a limited field of specialization, such as political science, law, economics, public opinion, or a particular nation, culture, or region. The decision-maker thus has the responsibility of synthesizing the advice, often conflicting, that he gets from these various specialists.

The research worker has to have more scientific knowledge than the average citizen, and consequently he is tempted to specialize in a particular aspect or region. Doubtless such specialized researches are important to contribute to the knowledge available for specialized advisors and for building a general discipline of international relations.

In my opinion, such a general discipline is important in order to concentrate in the smallest compass the knowledge essential for the average citizen and the decision-maker—and to make the specialist and researcher aware of the impact of international relations as a whole on his particular field and to warn him that the conclusions in his field are not necessarily adequate in themselves for either prediction or control in international relations.

I use the term "international relations" because I regard it as more comprehensive than "international politics." It covers international law, international organization, international economics, international communication, and international education, and also elements of geography, demography, technology, sociology, psychology, and ethics. In the absence of knowledge of these disciplines, international politics is likely to confine its view of the world to the balancing of military power, which has dominated thinking and practice in the last few centuries, but which modern technology may be relegating to the dust bin of history.

It has been common in recent years to contrast realistic with idealistic approaches to international politics to the detriment of the latter. "Realism" has sometimes meant emphasis upon past formulations without consideration of changing conditions. It has sometimes meant insistence upon the effectiveness of military power without consideration of the evidence that such insistence has often led to arms races, decreasing the security of all the participants.[1] It has sometimes meant emphasis upon what appear to be immediate necessities without consideration of the possibility, or even probability, that exclusive attention to the short run may frustrate long-run goals. It has sometimes meant concentrating on national or regional interests and overlooking the probability that, in an interdependent world, general stability that requires a world orientation, may in fact be the major national and regional interest. It has sometimes meant attention to how makers of foreign policy actually behave, although those who have been engaged in that activity report that so many decisions appear to emerge from accident or thoughtless response that such a narrative is meaningless. Louis Halle, who served for some time on the foreign-policy planning staff of the State Department, reports that the Point Four program was adopted because of a demand from the White House for something new to put in a pending speech; the demand resulted in the hasty unearthing of a previously rejected suggestion from a lower official which had never been discussed or developed. Later when President Truman was asked where Point Four came from he said it had long been in the air. Doubtless it had, but examination of its historical origin threw little light on why it was in the air. As Halle points out, the writer or teacher on international politics must construct conceptions from a knowledge of the atmosphere as well as of the event if he wants to be intelligible and meaningful. The facts in themselves do not disclose their significance.[2]

Reality in any of these senses must, therefore, be combined with ideas and, indeed, with ideals if it is to contribute to an understanding of international politics. Consideration must be given to the potentialities of the future as well as to the experience of the past. Appeals to reason must be considered as well as appeals to force and threats. Attention must be given to long-run goals as well as to short-run requirements. The needs of the world must be appreciated as well as the needs of the nation or the region. The decision-makers' comprehension of the atmosphere of opinion and their subconscious motivations must be considered as well as their actions. Exclusive attention to such potentialities and influences may of course lead to a utopianism so remote from the actual, the probable, or even any possible, world as to contribute little to an understanding of international politics, although even utopias may influence opinion in regard to long-run goals, as did Sir Thomas More's Utopia and many others examined in Lewis Mumford's *History of Utopias*. It makes a difference in international politics whether dominant opinion wants world stability and peace, national dominance and prestige, prosperity and enjoyment of life, spiritual contentment and disengagement, or the brotherhood and dignity of man.

TOWARD A UNIFIED DISCIPLINE OF
INTERNATIONAL RELATIONS

Even though it would have important uses, can a general and unified discipline of international relations with both predictive and control value be developed? The magnitude of the task can hardly be exaggerated.

Such a discipline should be based on a conceptual scheme simple enough to be comprehensible to the common man but realistic enough to be of explanatory value for the past, to have control value for the present, and to have predictive value for the future. To accomplish these ends the discipline would have two formulations, the one as pure science, the other as applied science, related to each other as, for example, physics is to engineering and physiology is to medicine.

To accomplish this a discipline of international relations must be cognizant of the professional and scientific disciplines that have been of service in the past and of their relations to one another. It must also present a realistic image of the world and of the major actors in it that is so appreciative of the major goals and values of nations that it can be generally accepted. The absence of such an image today is demonstrated by the differences between the images of a country in the mind of its people and in the minds of the people of other countries as reflected in their papers and journals. The image of the United States reflected in the American press has little resemblance to that presented in the Soviet and Chinese press; and the self-images of the Soviet Union, of China, of North Vietnam differ radically from the American images of these countries. Similarly, the image of the world, past, present, and future, in the various countries and indeed in different parties in the same country exhibits great differences. One is tempted to say that international relations in practice involve not relations between nations but relations between false images of nations in an imaginary world.

Peoples, nations, states, and governments that live in different worlds find it difficult to communicate with one another to reach agreements and to settle disputes. As Kurt Lewin has pointed out, policies are made and decisions taken on the basis of the world that exists in the mind, the "life-space" as Lewin calls it, not with the world as it may exist for an impartial and omniscient observer. Wars, as the UNESCO constitution says, are made in the minds of men.

The inconsistency among these various worlds arises because images exist, and must be developed, in a world continuously changing in response to human decisions, as well as to technological, economic, demographic, geographic, and other conditions. The image of the world is a reflection not only of what can be observed but also of what is desired. Realists in international politics often decry this situation and, as I have noted, seek to develop an image of the world as it has been, with insufficient realization that the important image is that of the world as it is about to be, and that in a voluntaristic world what is probable is influenced by human desires, and activities to realize them. The world as, in the opinion of powerful nations, it ought to be cannot be ignored in making an image of the world as it is likely to be. Desires and expectations may influence future actualities, especially if formulated in "developmental constructs," to use Harold Lasswell's term. Different nations want to make different worlds; and, as Justice Holmes once wrote, war seems inevitable "between two groups that want to make inconsistent kinds of worlds"[3] unless, as he said elsewhere, all observe toleration in recognition of the fact that "every year if not every day we have to wager our salvation upon some prophecy based upon imperfect knowledge."[4]

This conclusion makes it clear that in human affairs, particularly in international affairs, science and propaganda are interrelated. The natural scientist can develop formulas for predicting the motion of planets and atoms, confident that those objects will not listen to his prediction and change their motions accordingly, but social scientists cannot have the same confidence. Their predictions about the future of nations and of the world may change the behavior of these nations and make the generalizations on which the predictions were based invalid. Social scientists cannot ignore this feedback and so must ask themselves, "Will my prediction influence behavior toward a desirable or an undesirable world?" Inasmuch as social reality springs in considerable measure from ideas, as Plato taught, social scientists may have to follow Plato in publicly stating "noble lies"; the Bible in refraining from "spreading pearls before swine"; and René Descartes in withholding publication of his essay setting forth his objective image of the universe, which he feared, judging from the experience of Galileo, might be considered dangerous by ecclesiastical authorities. If they write in a technical jargon that only the elect can understand they may avoid this difficulty.[5]

The close relationship of science and propaganda is emphasized in our age of almost instantaneous communication of both events and opinions, of both facts and propaganda. The assassinations of President Kennedy and later of Lee Harvey Oswald were both seen and heard everywhere at the moment they occurred, and the varied interpretations of these events were widely communicated very soon after they happened. So also the dethronement of Premier Khrushchev, the atomic explosion in China, and the victory of the Labor party in England in the fall of 1964 were immediately known and speculated about everywhere. The varied and conflicting opinions about such events, which immediately spring up in different parts of the world, influence international politics much more than did the slower transmissions of news and more leisurely digestion of it by national opinions in past history. Today, unless such events can be rapidly oriented in a common understanding of international politics permitting a world opinion about them, they are likely to result in conflicting opinions augmenting the distorted images that plague international politics. A unified discipline of international relations would contribute to such an understanding.

It therefore appears that a realistic image of the world as it is becoming must synthesize knowledge of its past with knowledge of the developmental constructs that describe a world deemed desirable by the major governments and that guide their decisions. A discipline of international relations must seek to construct an image of the world that all peoples can accept because it is both feasible, in terms of past and present trends, and reasonably consistent with the desires of the major nations. This consideration led international lawyers after the Thirty Years' War, and again since the present stalemate in the cold war, to accept, in Khrushchev's phrase, a world of "peaceful coexistence, of states with different social and economic systems," because they recognized that within its territories each government may create a society in terms of its preferred ideology and developmental construct, but that in the world as a whole no state can do that. A world wholly Buddhist, Christian, Moslem, democratic, capitalistic, or communistic is not likely to emerge in the foreseeable future. A common image of the world as a whole is, however, the price of peace; and this can be achieved only if each of the desired but inconsistent worlds is confined to a narrower area.

Conditions change, however. No conceptual structure or image of the world will last forever. Consequently, a discipline of international relations must have within it self-correcting principles. It must be able to incorporate the news, which every day discloses new conditions in the interdependent and dangerous world that science and technology have given mankind, and in which conditions and opinions change more rapidly than ever before. The student of international politics cannot rest on his oars but must continually reformulate his hypotheses. I suggest that what is needed as an approach to international politics is a general theory, as objective as possible, of international relations, and a developmental construct of the world as acceptable as possible to the major nations and policy-makers of the world.

SYNTHESIS OF THE DISCIPLINES OF INTERNATIONAL RELATIONS

In my discussion of international relations I suggested two approaches to the creation of a general theory: a synthesis of existing disciplines, and an analysis relating the present situation to a universal conception.

Each of the existing disciplines is based upon certain assumptions, most of which are not universally valid, although they are valid in certain circumstances. For example, writers on international politics as a scholarly discipline have usually assumed (*a*) that sovereign territorial states with conflicting policies exist in contact with one another, (*b*) that the major value of each is its own continuous independent existence, and (*c*) that the only reliable means available to maintain this value is self-help supported by military power and alliances. In analyzing these assumptions they have usually arrived at the conclusions (*a*) that international politics tends to assume the form known as power politics, in which military force and threat are the dominant influence; (*b*) that whatever stability the system has results from a balance of power sustained by the self-interested policy of states in ganging up against any one of their number that is becoming so powerful as to threaten its neighbors, thus always confronting the most powerful with such overwhelming power as to discourage aggression; and (*c*) that the stability of such an equilibrium tends to deteriorate through internal forces. The progress of military invention in certain states encourages ambitious leaders to try to break the balance; and as war becomes more destructive some states prefer neutrality to the pursuit of balance-of-power policies, with the result that occasionally small states are conquered by large neighbors. Furthermore, federations, confederations, and permanent alliances may be formed for defense or aggression, reducing the number of independent decision-makers and tending toward a bipolarization of power, necessarily unstable because overwhelming power cannot be mobilized against either pole if it engages in aggression. Furthermore, insofar as the balance of power maintains stability over a period of time, the growth of trade, interdependence, and civilization develops a sense of security among some states, inducing them to place civil liberties and economic progress ahead of military pre-

70

paredness and power politics. They become, as it were, sheep and easy victims to the wolves that remain. The effect of these tendencies has been to lessen the stability of balance of power systems. In most civilizations, after conditions of instability and destructive war have developed in a "time of troubles," efforts have been made to establish an effective reign of law by general consent; but they have failed, and the peoples involved have been conquered, as by Hammurabi in ancient Mesopotamia, by Shih Huang Ti in ancient China, by Asoka in ancient India, by Alexander the Great in the Middle East, and by Julius Caesar in the Mediterranean area and Gaul. The "universal state" consequent upon each such conquest has, however, itself eventually succumbed to internal corruption or conversion, or to the attack of external barbarians; and a new civilization has been established and has gone through a similar cycle, the stages of which are described by Arnold Toynbee as the heroic age, the time of troubles, the universal state, and the universal church.

These assumptions of international politics have had a measure of validity since the period of religious wars was ended by the Peace of Westphalia in 1648; but they were attacked by pacifists and humanists such as Erasmus in the seventeenth century, by the principles of the American and French Revolutions in the eighteenth century, by advocates of arbitration and disarmament in the nineteenth century, and by the Russian Revolution in the twentieth century. Both the French and the Russian Revolution led to long periods when international politics was dominated by ideological strife. Nevertheless, the balance-of-power principle, generally under the leadership of Britain, prevented world conquest either by leaders of revolutionary ideologies or by ambitious leaders such as Louis XIV, Napoleon, Nicholas I, Alexander II, the Kaiser, or Hitler, but generally at the expense of protracted war.

Writers on the art of war and the art of diplomacy have usually made assumptions similar to those of the discipline of international politics. But different assumptions with different ranges of validity have been made by writers on international law; international organization; international economics; international communication; international education; and the international aspects of geography, demography, technology, sociology, psychology, and ethics.

A synthesis of two or more disciplines has sometimes been effected. Thus international lawyers like Oppenheim have assumed the applicability of their discipline only if the balance of power is stable. Writers on international organization have sometimes recognized that effective international organization depends on a balance of forces, although a much more complicated one than the simple military balance usually assumed by writers on international politics. Writers on international economics have usually assumed the applicability of their discipline only if political leaders are guided by reason—a condition which, they recognize, often does not obtain as such irrational activities as power rivalries and war attest. Writers on international communication and education have also recognized that leaders are not always guided by reason, and they have indicated how their disciplines have been utilized both to create conflict and to create cooperation between peoples.

A synthesis of all these disciplines might be effected by utilizing those with the widest range of validity, perhaps such scientific disciplines as geography, demography, and technology—dealing with material conditions—and psychology, sociology, and ethics —dealing with human conditions. Such disciplines might define the more restricted ranges of validity of the practical international disciplines and arts. Some would regard as most fundamental the disciplines combining theory and practice, such as international communication, international education, and international deci-sion-making. The last involves both the scientific prediction of the consequences of alternative decisions in a given situation and the evaluation of these consequences in terms of national and interna-tional goals.

The difficulty of deciding which discipline is fundamental is a consequence of the continual feedback that so complicates all of the social sciences. There can be no clear hierarchy among these disciplines, but only a network of relationships. Among primitive peoples with unchanging technology and culture, geography and social psychology are probably most fundamental; but as the progress of knowledge has increased man's capacity to control his environment and his values, the arts of technology, communica-tion, education, and decision-making become more important. In spite of these difficulties, the effort to organize and synthesize the existing disciplines may contribute much to the development of a unified and comprehensive discipline of international relations to serve as a guide to international politics.

CONCEPTIONS OF THE WORLD

The facts of past international life as recorded in histories and biographies, those of the present as recorded in journals and news-papers, and both as recorded in official documents and statistical compilations might seem the proper basis for a discipline of in-ternational relations; but the facts thus recorded are too numer-ous to digest. Most things that appear in the news have some sig-nificance for international relations. It is necessary to select those that are most significant, and this ideally requires a theory elabo-rating a conception of the world valid everywhere and forever. Doubtless in a world of change no theory can be eternally valid, but in the contemporary world a useful theory of international

73

politics must be universal. A theory applicable to only part of a world in which from a single point communications can reach every part in seconds, and nuclear bombs can reach every part in minutes, cannot be the basis of a useful discipline of international relations. Unfortunately, it appears that some writers believe such a discipline can be constructed for the free world, whereas others believe such a discipline can be constructed for the Communist world, each world ignoring the existence of the other. Such disciplines are obviously useless for dealing with the major problems of international politics.

Among general conceptions of the world that have been, and to some extent still are, widely accepted, four seem to have been most important.[6]

The conception of the world as a *plan* has always been attractive, whether the plan is formulated in the mind of God and works itself out from creation to the Day of Judgment; or is inherent in nature, which determines the future by the past; or emerges through the historic dialectic of thesis, antithesis, and synthesis. Such a plan, whatever its source, assumes a determinism that denies the validity of human decision-making.

The view of the world as an *equilibrium* of forces controlled by sovereign states in a varying and unpredictable condition of stability or instability has frequently been accepted, most notably in modern history. This conception has offered no remedy for the periodic conditions of instability and war that have afflicted mankind most destructively in modern times. The equilibrium has been neither static, dynamic, nor adaptive, but has oscillated unpredictably and often uncontrollably.[7]

Many writers have conceived of the world as an *organization,* with the parts functioning in subordination to the whole, that is continually guided by interaction of the parts with one another and with the whole; and this view has had some support in prac-

74

tice in the nineteenth century and particularly in the twentieth century. Such a world has aspects of an equilibrium, but one that is much more complicated than the simple military equilibrium among sovereign states that is usually assumed by writers on international politics, because global forces are influential, as are the forces of law, economics, opinion, and military power.

The world as a *community* of human beings harmoniously and peacefully interacting because of common attitudes and sentiments, guided by reason, but free from external compulsion, has been the ideal of universal religions and ideologies from Buddhism to Marxism. The realization of any of these ideals for mankind as a whole does not seem imminent.

It would appear that each of these concepts has had a degree of acceptance and realization at certain times and places but rather as a "developmental construct" than as a concept suitable for a predictive discipline of international relations. Each might be the basis for an applied, but not for a pure, science of international relations, and each would be more effective if it could draw on a pure science, as the applied science of medicine draws on the pure sciences of physiology, anatomy, and parasitology.

THE WORLD AS A FIELD

For purposes of pure science, I propose the concept of the world as a field defined by Cartesian coordinates designed to express continuities of policy or value and of power or capability. The value field and the capability field are distinguished on the assumption that decision-makers operate by formulating and pursuing policies that relate their values to their capabilities. The major powers, alliances, and other systems of action of major importance may be located at certain points in this multidimensional field; this indicates their relationships to one another in terms of each of the selected coordinates. The value coordinates that have been selected represent dispositions from subjectiveness to objectiveness, from abstractness to concreteness, from manipulativeness to contemplativeness, from restrictiveness to liberality, from self-orientation to situation-orientation, and from affirmation to negation. On each of these coordinates, a position near the origin indicates neutrality or balance, and a position toward the periphery indicates an extreme in one direction or the other. These coordinates discriminate the criteria by which systems of action evaluate, perceive, act upon, identify themselves with, interest themselves in, and entertain expectations from the persons and other systems of action with which they are faced. Other value coordinates at a lesser level of abstraction might be selected; but, being more dependent on a particular state of opinion, they would have a more restricted applicability. Those selected resemble Talcott Parsons' "pattern variables," which he believes constitute basic elements of value, combinations of which account for more concrete value systems, such as those characterizing the various civilizations, religions, ideologies, nationalities, and legal systems.

The capability coordinates manifest continua from energy to lethargy, from flexibility to rigidity, from cooperation to isolation, from strength to weakness, from wealth to poverty, and from technological advancement to technological backwardness. Here, also, one might select more concrete continua dealing with particular elements of political, economic, social or intellectual capability; but the more abstract the continua, the wider their applicability.

Movements of systems of action in the field are influenced not only by the proximity or separation of the systems in values and capabilities (which induces relationships of conflict, competition, coexistence, or cooperation, and movements of divergence or convergence in the field), but also by the relationships in a particular system of action of that system's elements of *government* or operative organization, *state* or legal structure, *nation* or culture, and *people* or psycho-economic character (these relationships vary the direction of movement according to the element that exercises major influence).

Application of the field theory requires measurement of the values and capabilities of each system of action (to locate it in the field), an analysis of the relationship of various aspects of distance between systems, and an appraisal of the relative importance of the components of each system in influencing movements in the field.

The field theory is noncommittal about the long-run future of the world or the kind of future that would be desirable. Its object is prediction—within, say, a generation—rather than control; and it makes no commitment about values, although the influence of values on the movements of systems of action is given major recognition.

The concept of the world as a field was appropriate to the world of disordered variety perceived by the overseas discoverers of the fifteenth and sixteenth centuries and by the observers of the power struggles of Machiavellian princes during the same period, in contrast to the hierarchic world ordered by moral principles that is pictured in Dante's Divine Comedy and was widely accepted as an accurate concept in the Middle Ages. It is also suited to the contemporary world, in which science and technology alter conditions so rapidly that the unexpected alone is to be expected. It is, however, applicable, in theory, to any period of history in which several systems of action—whether cities, empires, states, alliances, churches, corporations, or individuals—with varying values and capabilities, are in contact and utilize their capabilities to achieve their values. This application may indicate whether the

77

trend at a given time, resulting from interactions of the systems with one another and of each with the whole field, is likely to be toward *conflict* and an emphasis on international politics, toward *competition* and an emphasis on international economics, toward *coexistence* and international law, or toward *cooperation* and international organization.

The multidimensional field with six value and six capability axes cannot, of course, be visually represented in three-dimensional space; but "imagination may picture a twelve-dimensional semiopaque cheese within which maggots crawl around, the larger ones representing states, with the government at the head and the people at the tail. They vaguely perceive each other as they approach, often changing direction in response to primitive instincts and urges, to sophisticated patterns and policies, or to deliberate appraisals of purpose and power."[8]

DEVELOPMENTAL CONSTRUCT FOR THE WORLD

The field theory has been criticized because it lacks an over-all value system and so provides no common guidance for statesmen seeking a better world but only explains how, in a given situation of the field as a whole, they are likely to act when each is guided by the values and capabilities of his state. To meet this criticism there is need for an applied as well as a pure science of international relations. Statesmen need a "developmental construct" for the world which will elevate them above maggots, give them a long-run image of a future and better world, and suggest appropriate means by which they may realize that image.

The four concepts referred to have in fact been such constructs. In Western history the generally accepted construct was first a *plan,* the goal of which was set by revelation or natural law; then it was an unstable *equilibrium,* the virtue of which was its indeterminism and the opportunity it offered to the bold and brave. Now it is an *organization* such as was suggested by Pierre Dubois in the fourteenth century; King George of Podiebrad in the fifteenth century; King Henry VIII of England in the sixteenth century; King Henry IV of France, Émeric Crucé, and William Penn in the seventeenth century; the Abbé St. Pierre, Jean Jacques Rousseau, and Immanuel Kant in the eighteenth century; and Alexander I and Nicholas II in the nineteenth century, and was partially realized by Woodrow Wilson and the statesmen of Versailles and San Francisco in the twentieth century. The ideal of a harmonious *community* of mankind has at all times attracted many, whether its outlines are traced by Buddhism, Christianity, or Islam; by the democratic doctrine of liberty, equality and fraternity; or by the Communist doctrine of giving to each according to his needs and demanding from each according to his capacities.

The political institutions and practices of the Middle Ages, which conceived the world as a cosmopolitan community ordered in accord with God's will as interpreted by the Church; those of the period of *imperialism,* which—after the turmoil of the discoveries, the Renaissance, and the Reformation—recognized the divine right of monarchs to carry out God's plan as revealed in the Scriptures or as discoverable by reason in the law of nature; those of the period of *nationalism,* which—after the American and French Revolutions—regarded each nation as self-determined and sovereign; and those of the emerging period of *internationalism,* after the experience of two world wars, have been based respectively on the underlying constructs of the world as community, as plan, as equilibrium, and as organization.

It seems possible that a "developmental construct" suitable for a long future might result from a synthesis of the four concepts discussed above.[9]

1. The construct should include as basic *plan* the system of

international law and should clarify the meaning of "peaceful co-existence of states" by clearly defining the prohibitions in the United Nations Charter of "the threat or use of force in international relations against the territorial integrity or political independence of any state or in any other manner inconsistent with the purposes of the United Nations" and of "intervention in matters which are essentially within the domestic jurisdiction of any state." There is need for procedural elaboration of the Charter requirement to "settle international disputes by peaceful means in such a manner that international peace and security, and justice, are not endangered"; of the requirement of collective action in case the United Nations "determines the existence of any threat to the peace, breach of the peace or act of aggression"; and of the requirement "to take joint and separate action in cooperation with the organization" to achieve "the self determination of peoples," "conditions of economic progress and development," and "universal respect for and observance of human rights and fundamental freedoms for all without distinction as to race, sex, language or religion."

2. Such a construct would include policies to maintain a more complex and more stable *equilibrium* than that of the traditional balance of power maintained by arms races, threats of force, and periodic wars to make the threats credible. One nuclear war would be one too many for civilization. Policies have been advocated and adopted by nuclear powers to stabilize the balance of power in the atomic age by maintaining protected launching bases and sufficient second-strike nuclear capability to deter a first strike by any of them, at the same time maintaining sufficient first-strike capability to make the threat to use it an effective support for diplomacy. This policy seeks the impossible task of making nuclear threats both incredible and credible. Deliberate nuclear attack, even by China, seems unlikely, although the announce-

ment by the United States of a counter-force strategy and the building of superiority in nuclear weapons suggests such an intention and have caused grave anxiety on the other side of the iron curtain; but, in any case, dangers of pre-emption, escalation, accident, and miscalculation remain.

A stable equilibrium, therefore, requires the elimination of military force or threat of military force as instruments of policy, by creation of conditions making any use of nuclear weapons incredible and any use of conventional weapons inexpedient except for defense against armed attack or in United Nations peace-keeping operations. Programs of arms control to facilitate general and complete disarmament would aid in establishing these conditions, but such programs are not likely to be accepted unless successful efforts are made to relax tensions and to restore a degree of confidence, without which no system of inspection is likely to be convincing. Cultural exchanges, international education, and increased trade and cooperation in social and welfare programs, to eliminate false images and mutual fears, might contribute to an improved atmosphere. If states adopted in the national interest policies of defense without provocation and conciliation without appeasement, progress toward these conditions would be likely.

3. The developmental construct should include the United Nations *organization* with universal membership; with improved legislative capacity to keep international law up to date by General Assembly resolutions, the activities of the International Law Commission, and the organization of diplomatic conferences to conclude general treaties; with improved judicial capacity to recommend on political disputes through the Security Council and the General Assembly and to adjudicate legal disputes through arbitration and the International Court of Justice; with improved executive capacity to organize collective security by

prompt issuance of provisional measures to stop hostilities, to determine, if such measures fail, the existence of any threat to the peace, breach of the peace, or act of aggression, and to utilize, if necessary, peace-keeping forces to protect investigating commissions and to police cease-fire lines, and military contingents from members to stop aggression; and with improved financial and administrative capacity to engage in peace-keeping activities, to contribute to the economic development of underdeveloped peoples, and to facilitate social, economic and cultural cooperation, through the Secretariat, the commissions and the specialized agencies.

4. Finally, such a construct should include increased awareness of mankind as a *community,* by encouraging states to punish international crimes such as genocide, war-mongering, and the fomenting of civil strife in other states; to maintain universal standards of human rights within their jurisdictions; and to accept regional and universal conventions giving force to these rights in law through procedures such as those established by the Rome convention of the Council of Europe with its Commission and Court of Human Rights. It should be understood that progress in this field depends on the consent of states and that respect for the domestic jurisdiction of states forbids intervention even by the United Nations to compel acceptance of any particular form of human rights, unless indeed violations are of such gravity that they shock the conscience of mankind and threaten the peace of the world. The United Nations and other international organizations, governmental and nongovernmental, can contribute to the realization of a community of mankind along with the community of states. Awareness of mankind as a whole is an interest of men everywhere in the shrinking, independent, changing, and dangerous world of the atomic age. Everyone must join the human race.

The wide differences in the economic, political, social, and value systems in different areas of the world will for a long time, perhaps indefinitely, make the independence of states and their peaceful coexistence the most important concern of international politics, and will give the rights of states priority over the rights of man. Yet states are human institutions, and their peaceful coexistence is unlikely if some regard others as less than human. An awareness of mankind and respect for the dignity of men everywhere is basic to an understanding of international politics.

NOTES

1. Lewis F. Richardson, *Arms and Insecurity* (Pittsburgh: Boxwood Press, 1960).

2. *Virginia Quarterly Review,* XL (Winter, 1964), pp. 11, 25.

3. Quincy Wright, *A Study of War* (Chicago: University of Chicago Press, 1942, 1965), p. 738.

4. Quincy Wright, *The Study of International Relations* (New York: Appleton, Century, Crofts, 1955), pp. 18, 516.

5. *Ibid.,* p. 408, 509.

6. *Ibid.,* p. 485 ff.

7. *Op. cit.* note 3 above, p. 387 ff.

8. *Op. cit.* note 4 above, p. 546.

9. *Ibid.,* p. 1326 ff., 1528 ff.; Quincy Wright, "Maintaining Peaceful Coexistence" in Wright, Evan and Deutsch, eds., *Preventing World War III* (New York: Simon and Schuster, 1962), p. 410 ff.

The Representative Function in Western Systems

DAVID B. TRUMAN

No specialized professional competence is needed to observe that over the past half-century, and especially in the years since World War II, parliamentary assemblies have become less and less important as legislatures, in the strict sense. However much or little the forms have changed, legislatures have declined in significance as agencies assuming the chief role in designing projects of law and in enacting law. The phenomenon has been evident in Britain for a long time. In France, of course, even before the Fifth Republic, the institution of the government crisis and related practices have not wholly disguised the fact that public policy— when it could be identified—has borne the strong stamp of the executive and especially of the bureaucracy. Even in the United States the Congress in a few short years has moved toward a quiet acceptance of the executive as the principal source of its agenda and of at least the initial formulations of statutory proposals.

Political scientists in the United States might have been expected to concern themselves with this tendency more than they have. It has been noted, of course, and it is a largely implicit assumption underlying much of the work of recent years; but, perhaps especially in studies of the American system and commentaries on various of its aspects, explicit attention to it has been rare. Charles Hyneman has been an exception among political scientists in devoting attention to this tendency, and one can think of others, but they are few.[1] Many reasons for this relative neglect might be proposed. In the first place, American political scientists, especially in the last three decades, have carried on a love affair with the presidency and with the administrative side of government and only recently have begun to show reduced ardor. Secondly, the tendency under discussion has been less evident in the United States, since the Congress, despite significant changes in its role, retains more of the attributes of a legislature in the narrow sense than does the national assembly of any other major power. Thirdly, it may be that the tendency, especially in this country, has been in such measure a by-product of developments in substantive policy which can be regarded as functional for the system as a whole that its possible implications have been largely obscured. Some of these policy developments have been almost purely domestic, but at least an equal number have been associated with the critical necessities of national security and the acute interdependencies of the world that has emerged in the past two decades. These three circumstances may not fully account for our relative indifference to the matter. They certainly do not exhaust the range of possible explanations, and I shall want to return to them and others at a later stage and for a somewhat different purpose.

To attempt to account for the "nonlegislative" tendencies of parliamentary assemblies is even more hazardous and necessarily a good deal more speculative. Many factors are peculiar to particular countries. In France the ancient and traditionally antirepublican institution of the bureaucracy has been more than ready to assume power and initiative either with a dominant political executive or in the executive's place when unstable coalitions have made clarity and decisiveness impossible of achievement through either government or parliament. In Britain, where the genetic code of parliaments included only recessive genes for legislation in the strict sense, the emergence of a contemporary party system and the mutually complementary needs of ministers and career bureaucrats have combined to insure that Parliament's role in the design and enactment of public policy would be increasingly marginal. In this country, as Samuel P. Huntington has pointed out in a recent essay, a growing insulation of Congress from the more dynamic and dominant sectors of the society and a marked dispersion of power within the national legislature have been associated with a decline in the strictly legislative functions of the Congress.[2]

The tendency for legislation as a function to shift away from national assemblies can scarcely be regarded, however, as a general pattern produced entirely by factors unique to each national setting. Influences common to all obviously are at work. One of these is so familiar as scarcely to require mention—the technicality and the contingent character of a vast range of contemporary problems, which have inevitably shifted to the bureaucracy not only responsibility for a great proportion of implementing policy but also, and partly in consequence, the initiative for much subsequent legislative policy. In the United States especially, but significantly in other Western nations as well, this reflects a change in the salience and complexity of the political process itself. At least until World War I ours was a relatively simple politics, in the later years threatened but not yet burdened by the problems of a postindustrial society. The aggregation and accommodation of conflicting interests was accomplished, with one conspicuous exception, easily; and the legislature was not merely a channel but also the major locus of innovation in the governmental structure. Our comparative isolation from the mainstream of international politics accentuated this characteristic, but it is not unreasonable to say that we differed from the other representative systems of the West more in degree than in kind. In the heyday of the legislature throughout the West the matters that received their shape in its chambers were of far less, and less immediate, importance for the system and for the world than those that today come before it with solutions largely preshaped and awaiting criticism, amendment, ratification, and legitimation by parliamentary action.

In the years since World War II the prominence and complexity of international politics, especially but not exclusively for the United States, have provided another major force toward removing the legislative function from parliaments. If one takes "international politics" in a broad sense, this influence is nowhere more sharply illustrated than in the supra-national politics of western Europe. Stimulated by the East-West conflict and fostered by the Marshall Plan, NATO, and related efforts, the development of European institutions has been significantly and perhaps irrevocably nonparliamentary. The new institutional forms have, of course, imposed limitations on the national parliaments; but in addition the "parliamentary" organs within them have been almost wholly ornamental. European institutions, in the words of Karl Dietrich Bracher, have had the effect of "shifting politics from the parliamentary level to that of administration and bureaucracy."[3] Initiative lies, and is likely to remain, with national executives, including bureaucrats, and "European" technicians. (In this light one can understand, whether or not one agrees with, the critics in Britain who oppose her entry into the Common Market in part because it contains no significant role

87

either for the Parliament in Westminster or for any other. They are reacting, however shortsightedly, to a broad and fundamental problem.)

What is true of the new European institutions is not fundamentally different, however, from the network of international politics generally. The insistence and the growing complexity of a crowded world have denied to parliaments the legislative function in the nascent community. If for no other reason, the howling mob that in quieter and simpler times appropriately could be called the family of nations has compelled executives and bureaucrats to assume the initiative, including the legislative initiative, in an area that makes any distinction between domestic and foreign policy almost meaningless.

This brief and necessarily inadequate sketch of some factors contributing to the decline of parliamentary assemblies as legislatures in the strict sense carries the implication of inexorability and irreversibility. I cannot see how it or even a fuller account could do otherwise. But that is not the focus of my concern. It would be foolish and futile to ask political scientists to play Canute to this tide. My colleagues would be too wise, even if I were not, to try to resist or even to deplore change in a segment of the governmental apparatus that so apparently reflects inescapable realities in contemporary life.

My reason for suggesting that political scientists might concern themselves more fully and more explicitly with this tendency can be put in various ways, but they all boil down to one question: "What, if any, are the options—or, in more analytic terms, the functions—that may be narrowed *in the governmental system as a whole* by this tendency?" I say "if any" and "may be narrowed" out of a prudent respect for the canons of responsible inquiry, but I would not raise the question if I did not feel that the narrowing is at least a likelihood and that these functions are of more than casual consequence to the system.

At the risk of banality, let me try to explain what I mean. It has, in the first place, something to do with the values—or, to use a safer term, the variable consequences—of representation. The philosophical positions underlying various views of representation are, I am aware, numerous and not always compatible. I do not propose either to deal with them or to attempt to reconcile them; but I think it is a reasonable suggestion that one reason for the relative neglect of the tendency I have sketched is that, in a few decades, we have abandoned the assumptions of rationality and of the perfectibility of man that underlay the defense of representation, especially its popular defense, perhaps, but also its defense among the intellectuals. In the works of Woodrow Wilson, Charles Beard, or even, in some moods, Charles Merriam— to mention only three—you will find these assumptions virtually intact. I do not plead for lost illusions; I rather ask whether, assuming nonrationality in some Lasswellian sense and the infinite corruptibility of mankind, there still is not something at stake in the decline of legislation by representative assemblies that is functional for an order based upon universal suffrage.

What is that functionality? It may have something to do with legitimacy. I should agree, to the extent that legitimacy is not viewed as an objective attribute of the system but is treated rather as a widespread and recurrent psychic event; but legitimacy, even in this sense, is a resultant, one indicator of whether the functionality I refer to has been lost. It does not help much in thinking about the process by which the legitimacy of the system is strengthened, maintained, or undermined.

In the present context that process has more to do with the characteristics, the skills and outlooks, of those using power within the system than legitimacy suggests. One version of this point is the suggestion in various forms, sophisticated as well as suburban uplift, that the decline of assemblies as legislative bodies would be reversed if appropriately specialized and technically competent men were nominated and elected to legislatures. But is it the case, as this implies, that what is lacking or threatened *in the system as a whole* is technical, subject-matter expertise? If so, then it might be much simpler to let the initiative drift toward the bureaucracy and to encourage parliamentary bodies and other elected agencies to become merely ratifying units made up of nontechnical amateurs.

An alternative implication of this demand for increased technical competence in parliamentary assemblies is more suggestive. It is that what is sought is less the quality of substantive expertise per se than a situation in which two comparably competent sets of men confront each other and one of them is obliged to seek a renewal of its franchise from a mass electorate. On the narrowest of grounds, the argument is that in an order based on universal suffrage, with all that implies, an inescapable precondition of the stability of the political system is that an appropriate (meaning "unknown" or "undetermined") number of government actors combine with some degree of substantive, technical competence a special skill. This is skill in assaying what is asked or done in the name of substantive expertise and in reconciling or combining such claims or acts with the feasibilities that exist or can be created in the electorate, in the extragovernmental world in all its configurations. This is not a skill that exists *in* an electorate or its composite elements but one that is or can be developed in the heat that an electorate and its various publics can generate.

This is the skill that lies at the heart of the representative function in popular governments, almost regardless of what other attributes or normative features are assigned to it. This, it seems to me, is the skill that may be in jeopardy from the tendency that I am discussing. It is the primacy of aggregative politics and its functionality for the system that may be at stake.

The point is effectively analyzed by Richard E. Neustadt with reference to the United States, where it has paradoxically a special salience.[4] Taking as his point of departure the emergence in the 1940's of an officialdom whose scale and capacity for survival are unlike anything seen before in our governmental system, he argues that "the feel for feasibilities across the board of politics" that is peculiarly the capability and the contribution of the elective politician is under severe strain both in the White House and in Congress. Noting the increasing capacity, especially in the area of national security, of experienced officials to work effectively across divided jurisdictions, he suggests that if this trend should continue on a wider front we risk losing what elected politicians, President and Congress alike, "uniquely bring to public policy." Neustadt's immediate focus is the insufficient awareness of common stakes by President and congressmen, separated in our system by barriers that are partly constitutional but also and perhaps more strongly political, attitudinal, and semantic. But the problem in its generic elements seems to extend far beyond the United States and the special complications created by our forms and practices. Extreme though the case may be, the experience of Germany from 1930 through 1933 is not a reassuring precedent for a future enfeebling of the power of elected politicians. Nor, I submit, are the prospects for the Fifth or Sixth French Republics.

This view calls into question the familiar enthusiasm for "representative bureaucracy." It suggests that, in our justified insistence that administration *is* politics rather than a different kind of public activity, we may have paid insufficient attention to the possible differences between the roles, skills, attitudes, and perceptions of elected politicians, on the one hand, and those of bureaucratic politicians, on the other. How sure can we be that the bureaucratic politician's sense of the political system and its requirements is not so different in degree—in range, in complexity, and in immediacy—from the elected politician's as to be profoundly different in kind? Even if we could agree that this difference exists, it might be argued that the requirements of the representative function could be adequately met by arrangements in which elected politicians, in and out of parliamentary assemblies, either ratified or vetoed, as their collective judgment required, legislative projects originating elsewhere. But one might still wonder how long such a relation could persist effectively. Can the primacy of aggregative politics be maintained indefinitely in a system of popular government if for decades it is cut off from the legislative function, in the strict sense?

I should emphasize at this point that I am talking about a problem, about a tendency that raises questions deserving our professional attention. I am not discussing or asserting a fact. And I should repeat that I am not launching a "save our legislatures" drive. Rather I am asking that research and analysis be directed at the function with which I am concerned, but *in the system as a whole*. Can we determine how and under what conditions the elected politician's sense of the system differs from that of other politicians? Can our curiosities fruitfully extend to the questions of where, in what forms, and with what trends and what consequences such distinctive skills and perspectives of the elected politician are operative within a system?

I have sketched this problem as one that affects, presumably, all the developed Western countries and not simply because examples from this wide area readily suggested themselves. Much of the research must certainly be done comparatively, if only to increase the number of cases, despite the difficulties that this will encounter. As a profession political science has never been quite certain of the terms in which comparisons can best be made; and, outside of Britain and the United States, systematic study of national parliaments is, as a French scholar recently acknowledged, in an "embryonic stage."[5] In this country we may not be very far beyond that stage, but in the past few decades so many promising research developments have taken place that it may not be premature to advocate serious research on a problem as difficult and inclusive as this one. We have begun, for example, to follow the suggestion Hyneman made thirty years ago of studying systematically the relevant characteristics of legislators and other political actors.[6] We are more at home with research on political attitudes and on roles and perceptions of role.[7] Systematic, empirical work on various aspects of the representative function has been undertaken, as in the Survey Research Center's study based on the 1958 elections.[8] Somewhat more sophisticated advantage is being taken of the American states as an arena for significant comparative study, and certainly it would be wise to include comparative analysis at the state, and even the local, level in an attack on the problems of the representative function.[9] We are becoming somewhat more adept, in case studies of particular policies and policy areas, at examining a wider range of influences upon decision-makers and at drawing inferences to a wider reach of the governmental process.[10]

Finally, and perhaps most important, we are finding ourselves more frequently talking and thinking in terms of political systems as wholes, even when our immediate concern is with one segment of a single system. Our lack of consensus on the appropriate categories in which to analyze systems should not obscure the importance of this revived emphasis.[11] Even dealing with American data alone, however, and working in an environment that is perhaps unique in its receptiveness to and tolerance of empirical

93

political research, obstacles of the utmost difficulty face an attempt to deal with the problems of the representative function. Not the least of these is the key problem of making operational, of finding appropriate empirical equivalents for, the politician's skills of estimation and perception. It is a problem closely related to that of linkages, which V. O. Key wrestled with so stubbornly in his book on public opinion.[12] Equally difficult, if indeed within reach of research at all, is the problem of tracing the effects on public policy of the absence or presence of these skills. Perhaps these kinds of problems cannot be solved, but I wonder whether it is not important that attempts be made.

I realize that one of the objections likely to be raised against pursuing this line of research is that it is essentially policy-oriented and that in consequence it runs the risk of making premature inferences for institutional policy. This objection has weight. Over the years far too much writing by political scientists has been little more than partly informed, journalistic opinion-mongering.

If the direction I am urging were necessarily to lead to abandoning or weakening the search for hard data, for more sharply defined concepts, and for more powerful techniques of analysis, or if it inescapably were to substitute taking sides for or against the latest panaceas for systematic research and attempts at synthesis, I should abandon it without hesitation. Although I cannot feel that political science as a discipline can be strong unless it is also useful in some prescriptive sense, I also cannot feel that an area of study can become useful unless it is indeed a discipline, operating at a level above common sense and sufficiently self-conscious to be aware of its organizing assumptions, of the validity of its existing knowledge, and of the appropriate distinctions between insight and verification.

The problems of the representative function, it seems to me, are entirely compatible with, even if they may not be within the grasp of, a developing discipline of political science. They are not likely to yield to any but the most sophisticated methods, and they have the advantage of being broadly functional and system-wide in their relevance rather than confined to a single institutional segment. Thus efforts to solve them should strengthen the discipline as such as well as increase its relevance to the sphere of policy and experience.

NOTES

1. See Charles S. Hyneman, *Bureaucracy in a Democracy* (New York, 1950).

2. Samuel P. Huntington, "Congressional Responses to the Twentieth Century," in The American Assembly, *The Congress and America's Future* (Englewood Cliffs, N.J., 1965).

3. Karl Dietrich Bracher, "Problems of Parliamentary Democracy in Europe," *Daedalus,* Winter, 1964, p. 182.

4. Richard E. Neustadt, "Politicians and Bureaucrats," in *The Congress and America's Future.*

5. Alfred Grosser, "The Evaluation of European Parliaments," *Daedalus,* Winter, 1964, p. 153.

6. Charles S. Hyneman, "Who Makes Our Laws?", *Political Science Quarterly,* LV (1940), 556-81.

7. See, for example, John C. Wahlke, Heinz Eulau, William Buchanan, and LeRoy C. Ferguson, *The Legislative System* (New York, 1962).

8. See Warren E. Miller and Donald E. Stokes, "Constituency Influence in Congress," *American Political Science Review,* LVII (1963), 45-56.

9. The pattern was set by the work of V. O. Key, especially perhaps his *American State Politics* (New York, 1956).

10. See, for example, Bernard C. Cohen, *The Political Process and Foreign Policy* (Princeton, N.J., 1957).

11. Notably Gabriel Almond and James S. Coleman, *The Politics of Developing Areas* (Princeton, N.J., 1960) and Robert A. Dahl, *Who Governs?* (New Haven, 1961).

12. V. O. Key, *Public Opinion and American Democracy* (New York, 1961), chaps. 16-21.

Political Parties in
Western Democratic Systems

LEON D. EPSTEIN

I

My concern generally is with the problems of comparative study of Western democratic political systems. Parties provide the point of entry for an analysis that, I hope, will illustrate the general problems. The apparent universality of parties in Western democracies makes them a convenient as well as a significant subject, but I do not claim that parties are the only significant subject. One might examine interest groups or executive authority, for example, or a particular political function like representation, socialization, or rule-making.[1] Having been impressed with the observable differences in organization and function between American parties and European parties, I seek the explanation for such differences (and for any similarities) in the historical, social, and institutional settings in which the various national parties have developed. Eventually I hope to be able to say something about the political systems as well as about the parties operating within them.

This comparative study of parties was not, however, motivated merely by observable cross-national differences. Differences in this particular area relate to a pragmatic question of long and great concern to American political scientists. To reform parties as a crucial step in changing the operation of government in the United States has been an article of faith for an important school of thought in the twentieth century.[2] Often, although not often overtly, European and especially British parties have represented models for the American advocates of more responsible parties. Therefore, it seems to me that the comparative study of parties in Western nations can help us to estimate the validity of the suggested reform of parties in the United States. A political scientist need not apologize for this pragmatic concern. Our discipline, after all, is a policy science, the work of which should contribute ultimately to making judgments about our political institutions, even though the contribution may be indirect.

The primary effort in the study I propose is not to present new data but to arrange in meaningful relationships what has already been learned about particular parties. How meaningful these relationships can be is affected, in the first place, by the meaningfulness of the universe taken for analysis. Whether there is meaning in the conception of "Western democratic systems" as the universe for the study of political parties or other political phenomena may be questioned. For many scholars the conception is too broad because it includes nations too diverse to permit useful comparisons, and for others it is too narrow because it does not take advantage of the possibilities of generalizing from the experiences of the over 100 nations now in existence. In any case, it is hard to define "Western democratic" without seeming arbitrary.

Arbitrarily or not, I have defined "Western democratic" to include at least twenty nations. The twenty clearly Western-democratic nations are the United States, Great Britain, Ireland, Canada, Australia, New Zealand, Norway, Sweden, Denmark, Finland, France, West Germany, Italy, the Netherlands, Belgium, Luxembourg, Switzerland, Austria, Iceland, and Israel. A few of these provide almost no data. Nations that are marginal mainly because of doubts about their Western rather than about their democratic status are Japan, Greece, Turkey, and certain Latin American nations. Among the Latin American nations, Uruguay and one or two others would probably qualify on every count. Their exclusion can be justified only by the convention of treating all of Latin America as composed of developing rather than Western nations. Conversely, Israel is included as Western, despite its location, because it, like Australia and New Zealand, is regarded as an extension or geographic transplantation of Western society. "Democratic" is also used here in its conventional Western sense of free and open electoral competition for governmental offices. All of the first twenty nations now qualify according to this definition of "democratic." A few would not have been listed thirty years ago, although Czechoslovakia would have been. The democratic experience of any of these nations, plus some others, may be used illustratively with a freedom that would not be possible if we defined our universe more exactly for a largely statistical analysis.

There are other problems in any comparative study of Western democratic nations. The first is the national approach, which has characterized political science as it has history, out of which so much of our scholarly tradition comes. We have studied the politics of national units and we have tended to emphasize the distinctive features of each political system in terms of its own national background. The basic reasons for the national approach were good and virtually incontestable. Government itself is primarily national, and so are its related political phenomena.

As a result, however, political data and findings are so national in character as to render cross-national generalizing most difficult. The questions that have been asked about political parties in one nation are not often the same questions asked about parties in another nation. It is not surprising that the most justly famous "comparative" studies, like Tocqueville's *Democracy in America* or Bryce's *American Commonwealth,* are works written about a single nation other than the author's own. Then at least it is possible to ask questions about one nation that have meaning in terms of another.

The second limitation is closely related to the national approach. It is the divorce, notable in American political science, between American and European (or all foreign) subjects. Thus we have had many intra-European and intra-Commonwealth comparative studies, but hardly any Euro-American comparative studies. American specialists have usually remained in their area, and European specialists in theirs. The result is a remarkable absence of any generalizing about the politics of Western democracies that is broad enough to include the United States along with Europe.[3]

The third limitation is more basic, and it may help to account for the first two. Each of us has been limited in his access—linguistically, culturally, and otherwise—to the range of knowledge apparently necessary for broad comparative study; and most of us are not comfortable relying on the research of others, especially when others have not asked the same questions about their nations that we would ask.

Fourth, the highly promising cross-national survey research, represented by recent works of high quality,[4] has tended, like national survey research, to be limited to only some of the questions of concern to political scientists. Still, there can be little doubt that the whole conception of cross-national survey research, systematically asking the same questions in several nations, provides the basis for eventually reducing the barriers to fruitful comparative study.

The limitations still existing may be observed in works on political parties. Excellent works of various kinds have been written on parties in each of the major Western nations and in some of the minor ones.[5] The divergent questions raised by these national studies have already been noted. It is in the few but significant comparative works that special problems may be observed. The best-known major books are by M. Ostrogorski, Robert Michels, and Maurice Duverger.[6] Duverger's book commands attention because it is the most recent, and because it seeks a broader coverage of countries than does Ostrogorski's work and a wider range of topics than does Michels'.

Duverger's effort, by its very prodigiousness, best illustrates most of the difficulties of comparative studies. Seeking to transcend the national approach by citing data from other Western countries besides his native France, he has nevertheless produced a work that is distinctively French; the questions he asks about parties in other countries are essentially French questions. Thus one can understand his great concern with the election system and the number of parties. Also typical of the general limitations affecting comparative study is Duverger's Europeanism, which causes him to ask European, if not just French, questions about American parties. He is not alone among political scientists, European and American, who thus impose criteria derived from European circumstances to judge parties that have developed in response to different demands. That even Duverger's imposing learning and energy should suffer from limitations is discouraging.

II

I have not been discouraged enough to forgo a start on my own comparative study. And of course I have a national approach of my own. I concluded that such an approach was unavoidable, given the state of our training and knowledge, certainly of my own, and that I should be aware of the limitation and make allowances for it. My questions are American-inspired questions, and I hope that by being explicit in this respect I make it easier for European scholars to achieve their own balanced perspective.

A more obvious limitation of my work is its concentration on the parties of English-speaking nations, particularly Britain and the United States. Not only are studies about these nations most accessible to me, but my own first-hand research has been so largely confined to English-speaking nations that I am more confident about the relevance of illustrations from the United States and Britain (and, to a lesser extent, from Canada). This limitation may be so severe as to cause one to wonder why I have not confined my entire study to English-speaking democratic nations. The thought has occurred to me, but I have rejected it on several grounds. First, the English-speaking nations are a large enough part of the whole Western democratic universe to permit tentative generalizations from the fuller and more familiar illustrations that these nations provide. Second, there are available some useful works in English as well as in other languages on parties in continental European nations, and these can help to support or refute tentative generalizations drawn from the narrower base. Third, even if my generalizations have to rest almost entirely on illustrations from English-speaking nations, they can still be tested by other scholars more familiar with other Western nations. Neither I nor anyone else will regard my work as defini-

102

tive. Fourth, my concentration on explaining certain major differences between American and European parties makes it possible to use British parties, in a few broad ways, as European
prototypes without doing violence to the variations existing within
western Europe.

From what has already been said, it will be evident that my
method is to identify parties with similar characteristics in certain nations, and then try to find what other common characteristics these nations have to account for the similarities in their
political parties, as contrasted with other kinds of parties found
elsewhere.[7] Although the method is more impressive when many
nations (or other units) are included within the analysis, it is useful with as few as two nations and certainly with three. When
thus limited, our generalizations must be most carefully stated as
tentative or suggestive.

One other aspect of the method needs to be made explicit. I
usually treat parties as dependent variables. The main independent variables are general matters like constitutional structure,
degree of federalism, timing of mass suffrage, stage of industrialization, preindustrial social structure, and culturally based political values. As in most political analysis, there is unlikely to be
universal agreement about the classification of independent and
dependent variables. Many political scientists have treated parties
as independent variables, influencing the political environment
more than they are influenced by it. This has been especially
likely among party specialists, who have tended to glorify their
subject matter by regarding it as causal.[8] Clearly, party-reformers
do this because they intend to change the political system by
changing the parties. It has to be admitted that by turning this
around, regarding parties mainly as responses to circumstances, I
have tried to set the stage for a refutation of the party-reformers.

103

But no refutation is made unless I show how the circumstances, which I call independent variables, fashion parties in resistant forms. It is this demonstration that I hope emerges from my comparative analysis.

Before proceeding, I must define "political party." It means here, as it does in ordinary understanding, any group, however loosely organized, seeking to elect government officials under a given label. Having a recognizable label (which may or may not be on the ballot) is the crucial defining element. It is usual for such groups to have organized followings. So is it usual for them to have, or seem to have, principles and policies, although it is possible for a group without principles and policies or without an organized following to qualify as a party within my broad definition. Collective appearance, under a certain label, before the electorate is enough to distinguish a party from what might be only a parliamentary faction. My definition also enables us to distinguish parties from most interest groups, because the latter, although they often endorse candidates, do not ordinarily provide the labels under which candidates stand for election.

My definition can thus take into account all of the various groups that are called parties in Western democratic nations: major and minor parties, interest-group and broad coalition parties, long-established and ephemeral parties, highly organized and solely electoral parties, social-movement and nonmovement parties, principled and opportunistic parties, democratic and totalitarian parties (as long as they compete in a democratic system). No one of these types is "normal," but it is evidently normal for modern democratic societies to have parties of some kind. Whenever a nation extended the right to vote to relatively large numbers, parties developed (although in several nations they antedated the mass franchise). The presumption is strong that regularized labeling which parties provide became necessary when large numbers of voters had to choose among candidates whose personal qualifications they could not know and when candidates had to reach large numbers of voters, whom they could not know. It cannot be assumed, however, that the mass franchise or any other feature of modern democratic societies requires parties to do much more than the minimal labeling function. Only in some nations, not in all, have parties developed membership organizations or clear-cut doctrinal positions.

There is nothing universal about the number of parties, even of major parties, that exist in the various Western democratic nations. The matter of number is worth passing attention, although whether two or several parties seriously compete to elect candidates does not appear to be as fundamental and as important a classificatory device as much of the literature on parties implies. Two-party competition is not here regarded as a democratic norm or as a universally preferable pattern.

Continental European experience with multiparty competition is so extensive that we have in our universe of twenty Western democratic nations no more than six nations with long-term two-party competition—that is, with each party demonstrating its capacity to elect a majority of candidates sufficient to control the national government. The United States and Britain, despite the latter's persistent third party, are most clearly in this category. Australia, New Zealand, and Canada are conventionally counted. However, Australia has had a durable third party, whose support is necessary for a majority led by one of the two major parties; New Zealand now has a third party; and Canada has had several third parties that have substantially affected the achievement of a majority by a major party. The sixth nation is Austria, and it is even more doubtful. Austria has two major parties, but they have maintained a grand coalition government since World War II. Thus, they are not alternative governing parties in the usual two-party competitive fashion.[9]

Austria, it will be noted, is the only non-English-speaking nation to be included, even on generous terms, among the two-party nations. Only West Germany and one or two others might be counted as incipiently two-party. Surely this suggests that two-party competition cannot stand as a norm. If it is supposed to be the result of a "natural political dualism"[10] of opinion, the dualism is apparently natural only to English-speaking nations. If it is supposed to be the kind of competition necessary for strong government because of its majoritarian election results, the necessity is accepted in relatively few nations. On the other hand, these nations do bulk large in population, because of the United States, and in prestige as successful democracies. However, at least one fairly large country, France, has had multiparty competition for nearly a century; and although France's experience has been marred by the collapse of regimes, that has not been true for smaller multiparty nations—the Netherlands, Belgium, the Scandinavian countries, and Israel.

The universality and so the normalness of two-party competition may be questioned from another angle. Within our evidently two-party nations, even those so readily classified as the United States and Britain, some impressive exceptions are found. There are regional and local third parties, and there are many areas in which one major party so dominates over time that the national two-party competitive classification is inapplicable. These one-party areas may be whole sections or states; or they may be more limited urban, suburban, or rural areas forming constituencies wherein a given party's voters are clustered. The latter situation prevails in Britain, where about two-thirds of the parliamentary constituencies have been regarded as safely Labor or safely Conservative over at least two decades.

The American one-party pattern is more widely recognized. Its character in the South, when the Democratic dominance still retained its old staunchness, has been carefully described in one of the great books of American political science.[11] We are familiar also with long-time Republican dominance of certain Northern states. So frequently, in fact, has national two-party competition failed to find roots in large areas of the United States that intraparty electoral competition has been institutionalized through the direct primary. When this intraparty competition consists of clear-cut factionalism, it is virtually two-party competition. More often, however, intraparty factionalism has meant the personal and shifting politics that V. O. Key found in most Southern Democratic primaries.[12]

Primaries in one-party areas can provide fairly wide electoral competition as long as numerous voters, not just a relatively narrow organized membership, get a chance to choose the candidates to be elected under the dominant party label. Primaries may be inferior in other respects to the more closed methods of candidate selection, but at least they allow for electoral competition where otherwise there would be none that was meaningful. They are one kind of adjustment to the fact that under national two-party competition there are many one-party areas.

When one accepts the view that two-party competition is well short of being the usual Western democratic standard, there may be less point in concentrating, in cross-national analysis, on the number of parties a nation has. There is still some point, of course, since the number of parties at the national level in a given country may be importantly related to the nature of parties in that system.

III

There seem to me to be at least six significant ways to classify parties. I use dichotomous classifications for the sake of simplification, but I appreciate that within each classification a range of possibilities exists.

First, according to its manner of electoral organization, a party may be *skeletal* or it may have *mass membership.* The former consists only of a handful of leaders, including candidates for public office, plus a few retainers; the latter consists of large numbers of dues-paying followers in addition to the leadership group. A really large-scale patronage party, like the old American city machines, fits somewhere between these two extremes.

Second, judged by the way in which the important task of selecting candidates is performed, parties may be *open to voters at large* or *closed to all except organized members* (however many or few). The American primary is the clearest example of the open method; but even American conventions have often been relatively open affairs, especially when ordinary party voters elect the convention delegates. The closed method of selection, on the other hand, permits no one outside the essentially private party association to help choose candidates; association control may be national, regional, or local.[13]

Third, parties may be organized *nationally* or *federatively.* The local branches may be linked directly to the national party, or indirectly through state or regional units.

Fourth, parties may be *explicitly class-conscious* or *explicitly nonclass.* Chiefly, this refers to the contrast between the socialist working-class party (along with avowedly capitalist or agrarian

108

parties, which are often coexistent) and the party that, although middle-class in its leadership, seeks support of all kinds across class lines.

Fifth, there are *strongly programmatic* and *not so strongly programmatic* parties. Here no polar opposites can even be stated, since all parties claim some program, policy, principle, doctrine, or ideology. Yet certain parties are much more programmatic or doctrinal than others. The range in this area is from rigidly doctrinaire to highly opportunistic.

Sixth, in their governmental representation, parties are *individualistic* or *cohesive.* Candidates, when elected and perhaps even when they stand for office, may regard themselves as free agents in policy matters, owing no more than acknowledgment of the party label they carry. Or, at the other extreme, they may always accept the policy line of their party as that line is determined either by recognized leaders or by a caucus collectivity of which they are part. The first extreme of complete freedom from party is most unlikely.

I have no doubt that there are other typologies useful for various analytical purposes. These six happen to suit my purposes because they provide the basis for distinguishing between two party models: the American, and the generally European but particularly British. American parties are usually skeletal; their selection of candidates is relatively open; their structure is federative; their general character is explicitly non-class-conscious; their emphasis is generally nonprogrammatic; and their governmental representation is fairly individualistic. On the other hand, British parties (to let them serve as our European models) are mass-membership organizations; their selection of candidates is closed and private; their structure is national; they include at least one major party that is explicitly class-conscious; they are proudly programmatic; and their governmental representation is highly cohesive.

From this perspective, there are plainly ways in which the American model seems the less highly developed. Particularly in the area of organization, it is not surprising that both American and European political scientists have made this judgment. A skeletal organization, with or without patronage workers to man the precincts, is smaller, less elaborate, and less regularized than a mass-membership party; therefore, it appears to be a less highly developed form. The view of the American model as less highly developed tends to be confirmed by its other characteristics. Relatively open selection of candidates seems to follow from a skeletal organization; without a mass-membership base, the only "popular" means available is for voters to take a hand in the selection process. Even the American parties' federative organization, although it is connected to the federal system of government, looks less modern than the national organization of parties in a period of increasing centralization of governmental authority. A similar judgment appears to hold for the more individualistic behavior of elected officials in American parties, since it precludes as much effective action as an organized entity as is possible for a party whose elected legislators act cohesively. Less indicative of low development are the explicitly non-class-consciousness and the relatively unprogrammatic character of American parties, but even on these counts forceful criticisms have been made on the ground that a large working-class party committed to a socialist program represents an advanced state of development.[14] For the reasons previously cited, the American model might be regarded as less highly developed even if the socialist working-class party were left largely out of account. In either case, support appears to be given to the proposal that parties in the United States can and should become more like those in Europe.

One does not have to be an American chauvinist to question this argument. In what ways, aside from the most obvious one, are the less fully organized parties also the less developed? Surely the American parties are not less highly developed in the sense of belonging to, or responding to, a less highly developed social and economic order, and surely they are not less highly developed in the sense of being newer political entities. The fact is that American parties are the oldest democratic parties in the world. The United States, because it was the first nation to have a mass electorate, also had the first political parties, in the sense in which we now use the term. Europe has less experience than the United States with democratic political competition.[15] The later European parties could still be more modern than the American, just as the factories of a more recently industrialized nation are often more modern than those of an older industrial country; but that possibility would not clearly support the view that there are higher (more advanced) stages of development toward which parties inevitably tend. It might support this view if American parties, after an early, less highly organized period, began to resemble the European model. In the absence of such a tendency, however, it seems more likely that American parties are simply different from European parties in ways that cannot be expressed in terms of "higher" or "lower" stages of development.

This likelihood is strengthened by the realization that American parties were more highly organized in the middle and late years of the nineteenth century than they have been in the recent years of the twentieth century. The big-city political machine, in its heyday, was the largest, most elaborate, and most effective party organization we have known in the United States. When European parties were beginning to develop, American parties impressed observers as very highly organized—even as over-organized. Thus James Bryce described "the tremendous power"

111

of American party organization in the 1890's: "It enslaves local officials, . . . it puts bad men into place, perverts the wishes of the people, it has in some places set up a tyranny under the forms of democracy."[16] Equipped with relatively few principles, American parties, Bryce thought, had strong enough organizations to substitute for principles. No American, Bryce said, would dream of offering himself for a post unless chosen by his party.

Bryce's now unfashionable moral disapprobation of machines may have led him (as well as Ostrogorski) to exaggerate their power, but it remains undeniable that American parties of the 1890's were characterized by much more highly organized units than have lately been usual in the United States. This development, it should be emphasized, was relatively early in the history of the mass franchise in the United States. In fact, our city machines developed in almost immediate response to the rapid extension of the suffrage to masses of new immigrants. It is not far-fetched to suggest that this response was the American counterpart, mainly prior in time, to the European socialist working-class party, which organized newly enfranchised industrial workers. Nor is it outlandish, therefore, to suggest that a relatively high degree of party organization belongs primarily to the early stages of mass enfranchisement. The older American machines were closer than are contemporary American parties to the European model on these typological counts: the machines put more flesh, by way of organized supporters, on the party skeleton; they exerted more organizational control over the selection of candidates; and their elected representatives were likely to act more cohesively in legislative bodies. On the other hand, they were no more national or programmatic than contemporary American parties, and they were no more explicitly class-conscious (although their ethnic-group-consciousness may have been an American equivalent of European class-consciousness).

112

Both because of the early rise of the city machine and because of more general aspects of socio-economic and political development, which have been noted, it is necessary to search for a less simple explanation of the contemporary differences between the American and the European party models than that which regards the latter as the more advanced. Basically, my approach to this problem is to study the types of political parties as responses to different national circumstances, social and institutional, and to stress the importance of the circumstances existing at the time of initial development of parties in a given nation. The assumption is that parties, once started in a certain mold, are likely to persist in that mold even after the original conditioning circumstances have changed considerably. The parties, it is appreciated, can and do change, but slowly and not in all respects.

IV

In the present section and the next section of this paper I propose to summarize first the American and then the European circumstances that have provided the social and institutional molds for political parties and that therefore help to account for their characteristics. In the United States, for reasons already stated, the circumstances are especially those of the nineteenth century; and these have changed only gradually, as is evident when we discuss the *social and structural federalism* in which American parties developed. Even with a vaster area and many more people the United States of the twentieth century is a more highly cohesive national entity, socially and governmentally, than it was in the early days of the republic. Yet both substantial regional differences and substantial state governmental units remain vital enough forces in American life to continue to nourish the essentially state-oriented organizational basis for political

113

parties. Although we cannot be certain that the remaining vitality would now be sufficient to make parties state-based rather than national, if our parties were starting from scratch in the middle of the twentieth century, there can be little doubt about the original impact of the federal structure.

Another strikingly important and durable American circumstance is the *separation of executive and legislative powers*. No plainer difference exists between the United States and almost all other Western democracies than that which flows from the constitutional fact that the effective American executive is not dependent on a legislative majority for its continuation in office. The separation of powers appears to be the crucial circumstance in explaining the relative noncohesiveness of legislative representatives elected under a given party label in the United States. This noncohesiveness, or individualism in legislative voting behavior, we know to be a mark (although an exaggerated one) of American congressional parties; but a similar noncohesiveness is not uniformly characteristic of American state legislative parties. Thus we cannot conclude that the separation of powers is a *sufficient* cause for individualistic legislative voting behavior, but can argue only that the separation of powers *permits* noncohesive legislative parties in a way that the parliamentary system does not. The American government can and does work without continuous support by a legislative majority. The parliamentary system, however, cannot work at all well, given the modern need for stable executive authority, unless a legislative party, or a coalition of legislative parties, provides a consistent majority. In France and some other Western nations the absence of a cohesive majority in a parliamentary system has contributed to the collapse of that system. In the American system, however, there is no such drastic result from the absence of majority legislative support.

It seems likely that in a large and diverse nation like the United States each of two major parties would contain significantly diverse elements, whose cohesion, in legislative bodies or elsewhere, would have to be contrived; and it is contrived for certain limited purposes imposed by the American governmental system. Each congressional party is cohesive when it comes to organizing the legislative body; and, more importantly, each national party achieves a temporary cohesiveness every four years in order to try to elect its presidential candidate. Here the constitutional rules make it virtually necessary for a party to unite in order to achieve the collective benefits of power. No comparably strong institutional pressure exists—although there is assuredly some pressure—for congressional parties to be thus unified, certainly not continuously unified, as parliamentary parties tend to be.

A third American circumstance is the *largely pre-industrial and pre-urban environment* in which parties first developed. Some of their style was set by the Jeffersonian and Jacksonian eras, when white manhood suffrage brought forth political parties in a largely rural nation; and still more of their style derived from the middle and late nineteenth century, when the America of farms and small towns remained dominant despite the growth of industries and cities. In these respects, the United States was not unique. France, for example, was still relatively nonurban when modern parties developed in the Third Republic. The United States, however, was a good deal more rural when its modern parties began to develop. The point is worth emphasis, because we know that more highly organized parties have been essentially urban phenomena in the United States and elsewhere. Thus in a still largely rural America we should not expect the national parties to exhibit the high degree of organization that characterized the American city machines. Farm and small-town America might

115

have set the national style and then helped maintain it through various representational advantages that persisted after numerical superiority had disappeared.

A more specific, if negative, result of the development of American parties in a largely pre-industrial and pre-urban environment is that they occupied the democratic political arena before there was an economic basis for a large socialist working-class party. American parties secured the votes of large numbers of ordinary electors long before the electors were primarily industrial and urban workers. Republicans and Democrats had popular bases capable of expansion to include members of the new working class. That class, it is true, grew rapidly from both rural migration and European immigration; but American parties were accustomed to appealing to both groups regardless of class. The rural migrants to cities had always been enfranchised, and the European immigrants were given the vote as soon as they established citizenship (if not sooner). Thus a frustrated desire for political participation, which along with economic demands provided a basis for the European working-class party, had no reality among white Americans.

The free and prior gift of the ballot to the American working class does not stand alone in explaining the absence of a socialist working-class party. Another well-known American circumstance, the nation's *material wealth,* is surely relevant. The United States was such a rich and bountiful country, both before and after industrialization, that there was even enough wealth to raise the standard of living of the manual working class well above European levels. We do not have to ignore the disparities of wealth and income in American society, especially in the earlier stages of industrialization, in order to appreciate that the economic grievances of American workers were usually less sharp than those of European workers.

116

How much the widely believed-in *openness of American society* has to do with the nature of American parties, and especially with the absence of a large socialist working-class party, is less clear. We used to think that the frontier provided a safety valve for discontented workers, but this has been seriously questioned. So has the belief in a greater occupational mobility in the United States than in Europe. We now think that about the same degree of occupational mobility characterizes every Western industrializing society.[17] This leaves as a possible factor the high valuation placed in America upon openness. However intangible, this might well have constituted an impediment to the growth of class-consciousness and so to the growth of a large socialist working-class party. It is not just a matter of believing that one could move up occupationally. Also involved is the belief that this kind of mobility does not meet any really high social barriers. That, in turn, requires that the working class not be sharply separated or alienated from the rest of society. It seemed easier to avoid this separation in the United States because there was no pre-industrial tradition of a class society.[18] American parties exemplify American social values, or perhaps respond to them, by their broad electoral appeals and notably by their leaderships. These leaderships have always been heavily middle-class, including some members who were born in working-class families. At no time have important American party leaders been recruited in significant numbers directly from working-class ranks as they have been in European socialist parties.[19] Meeting the interests of the working class, as at least one major American party has done, did not require the class-consciousness involved in adopting working-class leaders.

Much has been made of an *American ideological consensus* in connection with the relatively nonprogrammatic character of American parties. Insofar as this consensus has meant less class-consciousness, it can be connected to the absence of one kind of programmatic party—that which opposes a socialist economic order to a capitalist one. Often this is what students of ideology are talking about. For them "ideology" means socialist ideology and consequently a meaningful party program. Consensus on the capitalist economic order, therefore, means that parties in the United States are nonprogrammatic. Although this definition of "ideology" is rather constricted, it probably has to be so if the term is to be used to distinguish the basis of American parties. If the concept is more loosely defined, as in the question of how much governmental intervention is ideologically acceptable, American parties do not seem committed to a consensus. Of course, when it comes to views on the fundamental governmental order, there appears to be the same degree of American consensus as there is on the general economic order. No basis for programmatic parties can be found in disagreements about the legitimacy of the constitutional system, but this is hardly the basis for programmatic parties in any stable democratic nation.

While in the area of intangible values, I should mention one other American circumstance related to the nature of parties. It is the *populist democratic tradition*. Perhaps "direct democracy" would be as good a phrase. What I am referring to is the American preference, unusual in degree among Western democracies, for reducing the barriers between voters and their elected officials. This has been expressed by the direct election of a host of state, county, and other local executive officers as well as legislators; and it has also been expressed by the direct-primary method of selecting party candidates. Generally it has meant a bias against party organization, surprising in a nation that has accepted high degrees of organization in so many other aspects of its life. To an extent, this populist tradition can be attributed to the rural circumstances that set the tone for American politics; but the

tem, is not at all limited to Europe. In varying ways, every Western democracy except the United States makes its working executive dependent on legislative authority both for election and for continuation in office. It is true that Switzerland operates a rather special variant of the parliamentary system and that France of the Fifth Republic has at least temporarily substituted a separately elected executive as the principal source of authority (yet without abolishing the traditional dependence of the working executive on the legislative body), but Canada and Australia are as clearly parliamentary as Britain itself.

In comparative perspective, the presence of the parliamentary system in Canada is especially significant.[21] The parliamentary system is associated with the existence in Canada of political parties that, in the vital characteristic of parliamentary cohesion, resemble British rather than American parties. Nothing else but the demands of the parliamentary system would seem to account for the British and Canadian similarity in legislative-party behavior. Other Canadian circumstances are much more like those of the United States than they are like Britain's or Europe's. Note Canada's intense social and structural federalism, the pre-industrial and pre-urban environment in which its parties originally developed, its material wealth, and its American-type ideological consensus. Admittedly, Canadian society seems less open and less populist than the American; but it is considerably more so than the European. Anyway, these circumstances would be difficult to connect with the party loyalty of elected legislative representatives. In Canada as in Britain, Australia, and every European nation with a working parliamentary government, parliamentary-party cohesion seems the response essential to make the system work.

As we return to more specifically European circumstances, it will save time to consider together those circumstances that seem related to the emergence of the socialist working-class party. These are the already considerably *industrial and urban environment* in which European democratic parties developed, the *material hardships* accompanying the early industrialization, and the *stratified society* carried over from pre-industrial times.

That European parties, in contrast to American parties, developed in a more heavily industrial and urban environment does not itself explain the socialist working-class party;[22] but it helps to supply an explanation when it is appreciated that in Europe not just parties but the suffrage on which parties are based came when large numbers of urban industrial workers were already present. In some nations, like Germany, the socialist party was the first major democratic party—the first party to appeal for the support, as well as to represent the interests, of the propertyless masses. Moreover, both in Germany and in the Scandinavian nations, as well as in some other countries, the socialist party existed even before the enfranchisement of urban workers and so took part in the effort to enfranchise what later became its following. In other nations, of which Britain is the best example, the socialist party did not quite precede mass suffrage, but it came along soon enough afterward to represent a newly enfranchised working class aware, as was the rest of the community, of its special status. That status, in Britain as elsewhere in Europe, derived from other facets of experience in addition to late enfranchisement. These were the economic squalor more widely characteristic of European than of American industrialization and the residual feudal sense of class identification that both manual workers and their betters carried into the nineteenth- and early twentieth-century societies from the pre-industrial age.

These circumstances together coincide, not surprisingly, with a kind of *ideological cleavage* that is another element making European parties different from American parties. The working class in European nations was sufficiently distinct to support a view of the nature of the economic order, and even sometimes of the political order, different from that held by the upper and middle classes.

The European circumstances noted in the last three paragraphs account for more than the existence of the large socialist working-class party. They also help explain the mass-membership organization that characterizes some nonsocialist as well as all socialist parties in Europe. The parliamentary system, let it be noted, is not a relevant factor here. Logically there is no basis for connecting it to mass-membership parties, and the coexistence in Canada of the parliamentary system (and cohesive legislative parties) with skeletal external organization supports the logic. But all of the circumstances associated with the development of a socialist party seem relevant to mass-membership organizations generally. The reasons for this may be that the socialist party itself is the prime exemplar of the mass-membership organization and that nonsocialist parties find it useful to imitate socialist organization in order to compete with it. This influence Duverger calls "contagion from the Left."[23] But the circumstances making for a highly organized, class-conscious, and ideological party on the Left may also directly make for the same kind of party on the Right. The upper and middle classes in Europe, when forming highly organized parties, may not have responded only to the challenge of the socialist Left. They may have directly responded to the same circumstances that produced working-class parties. Admittedly, the necessity for organizing dues-payers and for other forms of collective action would not have been so great as it was for the working class, whose strength lay entirely in numbers; but organization would still have been useful. More to the point, organization would have been possible on the basis of class-consciousness. The impressively large dues-paying membership of the British Conservatives, a class organization if there ever was one, provides an excellent illustration. Whether any organization of such magnitude could be built and regularly maintained without class-consciousness is open to doubt.

VI

Much of what I have described as accounting for the differences between American and European parties is historical. The parties are still different, but the differences in conditioning circumstances may no longer exist in the same degree. Obviously this holds for the pre-industrial American environment versus the industrial European environment in which parties first developed; and it probably holds for the difference in class consciousness between the United States and Europe, since a diminution in European class consciousness is widely believed to have taken place. But it is not true for the key institutional determinant flowing from the difference between the separation of powers and the parliamentary system. The results of this continuing difference in circumstances, plus the continuing habitual results of certain admittedly changing conditions, seem likely to maintain American and European parties as distinctive political phenomena. They have come to perform different functions in their respective political systems, and the systems themselves have developed in accordance with these differences.

Nevertheless, in the light of those circumstances that have changed or are changing, it is possible that American and European parties are becoming more alike in some respects. I prefer to put the point in this way rather than to adopt the more usual idea that American parties are coming to resemble the European or the unconventional idea that European parties are coming to resemble the American. I should be honest, however,

124

and confess that I lean toward the latter view. The major exception to this development is the tendency of American parties to become more national. Although they are a long way from overriding the governmental federalism which, with social federalism, made and keeps the parties organizationally federative, there is a good deal of evidence of the nationalization of issues, elections, and political personalities.[24] This nationalization has so far had surprisingly few counterparts in organizational growth at the national-party level, but the probability of such growth remains.[25]

In other respects, there are almost no signs of the Europeanization of American parties. None should be expected by way of complete legislative-party cohesion as long as European party cohesion is viewed primarily, as it has been here, as the product of a parliamentary system. Nor should any Europeanization be expected by way of mass membership, class consciousness, and more deeply ideological programs, as long as these characteristics are thought to flow from older and different (although now diminishingly different) European circumstances. The same can be said for any change from open to closed methods of selecting candidates, since the democratic prerequisite for the closed method involves a mass-membership party. Much, in fact, depends on whether the United States is developing mass-membership parties. Some observers might argue that such organizations are growing in the United States despite the absence of circumstances similar to those of Europe of the late nineteenth and early twentieth centuries. The argument would have to rest on the slender evidence of the party clubs that have developed in certain American cities and suburbs during the last two decades. So far, however, these clubs have not usually been as large as their European counterparts; they have been limited mainly to middle-class citizens in both major parties; they have been sporadic in most of the areas where they have existed at all; and they have been less high or-

125

ganized than the old city machines, which they seek in some instances to replace.[26]

Although the decline of the old machines based on a vanishing mass patronage might seem conducive to the growth of policy-oriented membership organizations, there are many countervailing forces in modern society that make the last half of the twentieth century an unlikely time to build parties along those lines. Among these forces, deserving much fuller treatment than is possible here, are the new mass media of communication and the accompanying public-relations and opinion-survey techniques. All are enormously expensive. They require large sums to buy communication time and expert personnel. No significant portion of the necessary money can be raised through membership dues, which have to be modest if there is to be a large membership; and no significant portion of the work can be done by amateur volunteers. In other words, membership organizations seem largely irrelevant to what has become the major campaign method for candidates and parties; and this method, principally employing television, is likely to become more important. It is the efficient way for a party, through its leaders, to reach masses of voters. Furthermore, it suits the increasingly educated mid-twentieth-century citizen, who, especially in the United States, is already organized in interest groups designed to influence governmental policy and who can enjoy making a choice between candidates and parties on the basis of personal appeals over his television set. Neither the old patronage organization nor the mass-membership organization is needed as it might have been in earlier democratic times.

If there are technological trends now working against the development of mass-membership party organizations in the United States, they should by now also be operative in Europe to reduce the importance of such organizations as have existed. Television,

public relations, and opinion surveys have in fact become prominent in European politics during the last decade or so. Their rise
has coincided with an unusually sharp change in many of the
circumstances that we have believed initially responsible for
mass-membership parties. Thus it is hard to say what would have
caused a decline in organized membership, but there is considerable evidence of such a decline—especially in Britain, Germany,
and France.[27] Not only are there fewer members now than in former years, but the parties that have depended on such member-
ships rather than on newer campaign techniques have not com-
peted successfully. The less highly organized conservative parties
have tended to pioneer the new style of politics and to be followed,
often slowly and reluctantly, by socialist working-class parties.
The contagion is now from the Right; and, in some ways, it is
from the United States.

NOTES

1. The best-known use of the functional approach is by Gabriel
A. Almond and James S. Coleman in *The Politics of the Developing
Areas* (Princeton, N.J.: Princeton University Press, 1960). The intro-
duction to their book presents a functional scheme derived from
Western models.

2. See Austin Ranney, *The Doctrine of Responsible Party Government* (Urbana: University of Illinois Press, 1954); E. E. Schattschneider, *Party Government* (New York: Holt, Rinehart & Win-
ston, 1942); James MacGregor Burns, *The Deadlock of Democracy*
(Englewood Cliffs, N.J.: Prentice Hall, 1963).

3. An important exception, in the field of voting behavior, is
Seymour Martin Lipset, *Political Man* (Garden City, N.Y.: Double-
day, 1960). Another is Robert R. Alford, *Party and Society* (Chicago:
Rand McNally, 1963).

4. For example, Gabriel A. Almond and Sidney Verba, *The*

Civic Culture (Princeton, N.J.: Princeton University Press, 1963) and Philip E. Converse and Georges Dupeux, "Politicization of the Electorate in France and the United States," *Public Opinion Quarterly*, XXVI (Spring, 1962), 1-23.

5. Apart from American texts, there are outstanding books like Robert McKenzie, *British Political Parties* (London: Heinemann, 1963 ed.) and Philip Williams, *Crisis and Compromise: Politics in the Fourth Republic* (London: Longmans, Green, 1964 ed.)

6. M. Ostrogorski, *Democracy and the Organization of Political Parties* (London: Macmillan, 1902); Robert Michels, *Political Parties,* trans. Eden and Cedar Paul (Glencoe, Ill.: The Free Press, 1949), first published in 1915; Maurice Duverger, *Political Parties,* trans, Barbara and Robert North (New York: John Wiley, 1954), first published in French in 1951.

7. My colleague, Herbert Jacob, has called the method "nonquantitative multivariate analysis."

8. This seemed especially true a decade or two ago. The tendency is not displayed in the very recent work by Frank Sorauf, *Political Parties in the American System* (Boston: Little, Brown, 1964).

9. H. Pierre Secher, "Coalition Government: The Case of the Second Austrian Republic," *American Political Science Review,* LII (September, 1958), 791-808.

10. Duverger, p. 215

11. V. O. Key, Jr., *Southern Politics in State and Nation* (New York: Knopf, 1950).

12. *Ibid.*

13. The power of local associations is stressed by Austin Ranney in his general study of British candidate selection, *Pathways to Parliament* (Madison: University of Wisconsin Press, 1965).

14. Duverger, pp. 4-5 ff.

15. A useful comparative chronology of suffrage extensions has been constructed by Stein Rokkan in "Political Participation," a paper presented to the International Political Science Association at its Paris congress in 1961.

16. James Bryce, *The American Commonwealth* (Chicago: Charles Sergel, 1891), II, 491-92.

17. Seymour Martin Lipset and Reinhard Bendix, *Social Mobility in Industrial Society* (Berkeley: University of California Press, 1959)

and David V. Glass, *Social Mobility in Britain* (London: Routledge and Kegan Paul, 1954).

18. Louis Hartz, *The Liberal Tradition in America* (New York: Harcourt, Brace, 1955), p. 234.

19. Donald R. Matthews, *The Social Background of Political Decision-Makers* (Garden City, N.Y.: Doubleday, 1954) and C. Wright Mills, *The Power Elite* (New York: Oxford University Press, 1956). The American data, showing a small minority of political leaders from the working class in both the nineteenth and the twentieth century, can be contrasted with the sharp change in Britain from a complete absence of such leaders in the nineteenth century to their presence in large numbers within the Labor party in the twentieth century. I have made this contrast in "British Class Consciousness and the Labour Party," *The Journal of British Studies,* I (May, 1962), 136-50. Full British data are now available in W. L. Guttsman, *The British Political Elite* (London: MacGibbon & Kee, 1963). Although exactly comparable data have not been found for other European nations, what is known about the social backgrounds of leadership in several continental nations tends to confirm the existence in those nations of the British pattern which associates working-class leaders almost exclusively with the rise of working-class parties. From research of my own, I have learned that Canadian leadership resembles the American pattern—just as Canada resembles the United States in not having a major socialist working-class party.

20. On the provinces as crucial Canadian party elements, see R. MacGregor Dawson, *The Government of Canada* (Toronto: University of Toronto Press, 1957), p. 529. On Australian federal party structure, see Aaron Wildavsky, "Party Discipline under Federalism: Implications of Australian Experience," *Social Research,* Winter, 1961, pp. 437-58.

21. I have argued this at length in "A Comparative Study of Canadian Parties," *American Political Science Review,* LVIII (March, 1964), 46-59.

22. There are the troublesome questions of whether the Labor parties of Australia and New Zealand are European-style socialist working-class parties, and if so whether they (especially the class-conscious Australian party) can be accounted for as the result of the transplantation of late nineteenth-century British workers.

23. Duverger, p. 25.

24. E. E. Schattschneider, "United States: The Functional Approach to Party Government," in Sigmund Neumann, *Modern Political Parties* (Chicago: University of Chicago Press, 1956).

25. American national party committees are hopefully described by Cornelius P. Cotter and Bernard C. Hennessy, *Politics without Power* (New York: Atherton Press, 1964).

26. The broadest study of the new clubs is James Q. Wilson, *The Amateur Democrat* (Chicago: University of Chicago Press, 1962). Reports may also be found in Leon D. Epstein, *Politics in Wisconsin* (Madison: University of Wisconsin Press, 1958) chap. 5; in Currin Shields, "A Note on Party Organization: The Democrats in California," *Western Political Quarterly,* II (December, 1954), 673-84; and in Hugh Bone, "New Party Associations in the West," *American Political Science Review,* XLV (December, 1951), 1115-25.

27. British Conservatives dropped from a peak of 2,805,032 members in 1953 to about 2,250,000 in 1961 (McKenzie, p. 187), and British Labor declined from a high of 1,014,524 individual direct-dues-paying members in 1952 to 767,459 in 1962 (*Report of the Sixty-second Annual Conference of the Labour Party,* 1963, p. 47). The German Social Democrats declined from their postwar high of 875,479 in 1947 to below 600,000 in the mid-fifties before rising to 623,816 in 1958; the French Socialist membership decline has been even sharper (data for both countries in *Yearbook of the International Socialist Labour Movement,* Vol. 2, 1960-61 [London: Lincolns Prager, 1960], 121-22, 130-31). Socialist party membership in most of the smaller European nations has been fairly stable in the last decade.

Problems in the Study
of Urban Politics

JAMES Q. WILSON

The principal problem in the study of urban politics is less with its means than with its ends. The journals and bookshelves are choked with articles and volumes arguing at white heat and in sometimes strident tones the "methodology" of urban political studies—arguing, in short, the means by which one should seek the answers to questions in this field. At the center of this controversy can be found the bloody but unbowed figure of Floyd Hunter; around him, his sociological defenders trade blows with his political-science attackers. Even to mention the controversy now requires a footnote of staggering length to refer the reader to the endless literature on this subject.[1]

I think this has gone on long enough. The methodological issue—how we study urban politics—is not a trivial issue; but it is not the fundamental one, either. It was a secondary issue when it was first raised, and it is a secondary issue now. The basic issue is not how we answer questions but what questions we want to answer; ultimately, we should be more concerned with where we are going than with how we get there.

131

We have been in danger for some time, it seems to me, of developing, at least with respect to urban affairs, a kind of "apolitical" political science. This is unfortunate, for I am sufficiently loyal to my own field to believe that political science, to a greater extent than sociology or economics (the disciplines to which we are most in danger of selling out), has had a fundamental preoccupation with the ends of human action. It is because of this preoccupation, indeed, that the study of politics in our universities has always included the study of political philosophy as well as the study of political facts. Although these two wings of the profession are often at war over the claims each makes, both have (or should have) one concern in common: the ends and outcomes of political action. Just as the political philosopher is properly concerned with systematically inquiring into the moral quality of political action (more than with the history of ideas), so the political empiricist is properly concerned with systematically explaining why political action has one outcome rather than another.

Various analytical concepts can be used to organize (or justify) political inquiry, but almost all of those in common use share this concern for ends. Politics may be the study of power, but a power relationship presupposes a difference in ends that a wielder of influence attempts to overcome. Politics may be the study of conflict; what is in conflict, however, are the goals of the actors. Politics may be the study of political development, modernization, or legitimacy; it is difficult to raise these issues, however, without asking why development, modernization, and legitimacy are important. The answer, it seems to me, is that each implies that government will serve some ends and not others, will distribute goods and services to benefit one group and not another, or will mobilize loyalty for one cause and not for another.

Not every political science study, certainly, need be considered unpublishable if it fails to explain differences in policy outcomes. One can list an imposing number of intellectually interesting questions that have no immediate or obvious connection with ends. Without discounting the value of studying such matters, I would argue that the traditions, the classic literature, and the special competence of our profession have always been, in mood if not in practice, ultimately concerned with the ends of political action. Social science seeks to explain human behavior; political science, whatever else it may do, at the very least seeks to explain why some ends and not others are served by the community and the state. "Who governs?" is an interesting and important question; an even more interesting and more important question, it seems to me, is "What *difference* does it make who governs?"

Norton E. Long called our attention to the importance of such research objectives in his article "Aristotle and the Study of Local Government."[2] Like almost everything else he has written, this essay was widely influential. At least, part of it was, for it now appears that his readers got only half the message. They certainly acted as if they had paid close heed to his suggestions that Aristotle, in addition to being concerned with the formal or legal constitution of the community, was concerned as well with its "economic" or "sociological" constitution—"the actual economic and social structure of the society that underlies and informs the legal constitution."[3] The more important part of the message, which seems to have been forgotten, was that the reason for this concern with the regime (now called the "power structure") was that the "regime exemplifies a particular conception of the good life, be it the wealth of oligarchy, the freedom of democracy, or the martial spirit of timocracy." How a city is governed, in short, should make a difference in what ends that city serves.

It is entirely possible, of course, that the character of the regime makes no difference at all in what ends are served; this would be a discouraging finding, to be sure, but nonetheless one of the greatest theoretical importance. No greater blow to both hot-blooded advocates of "good government" and cool-eyed defenders of machine politics could be delivered than to establish that, after all, procedures make no difference. (How the political philosophers would react is a matter of conjecture, but they are a hardy lot who may admire Socrates for drinking the hemlock but have no intention of trying any themselves.)

Many problems stand in the way of making meaningful inter-city comparisons. Nothing, it seems to me, is clearer than the fact that simple two-by-two tabulations relating easily specified variables will not get us very far. If they could, then performing some rank-order correlations among the tables in the *Municipal Yearbook* (perhaps throwing in material from the *City and County Data Book* for good measure) would answer our questions. Any graduate student could do it. But it is not simply because professors are unlikely to admit that any graduate student could do their work that such procedures are, by and large, blind alleys. Political events are too complex for any single variable (or any two variables) to explain very much, particularly since we are dealing with cities that are all part of one nation and, broadly, one culture. (Cultural uniformity is both a blessing and a curse: on the one hand, it makes it possible to "hold constant" many variables while looking at a few critical ones; on the other hand, it reduces —perhaps eliminates—the variation in those variables we do examine.)

Comparative analyses of urban political systems are hard precisely because it is so difficult to specify outcomes. We have become fairly sophisticated about inputs: we have studied the distribution of influence, forms of government, city ecology, and party organization. But we have only begun to suggest what it is that cities *do* that might be affected by these inputs. James Coleman, Maurice Pinard, and others have begun to analyze the incidence of water-fluoridation among various kinds of cities in a way that suggests that the character of the city's regime may have a considerable influence independently of the distribution of preferences among the citizens.[4] Amos Hawley has offered some data concerning the adoption of urban-renewal programs that have the same implication, although his findings are being questioned by some other sociologists.[5] Oliver P. Williams and Charles R. Adrian, in the most ambitious effort thus far to relate regimes to outcomes, have shown some important policy variations—in four middle-sized cities in Michigan—that depend on community differences.[6]

These efforts have not been completely successful. There are several reasons for this, all of them indicative of the difficulties inherent in comparative analysis. Most importantly, the available data on city "inputs" and "outputs" are not readily comparable without extensive reworking. One might assume, for example, that a city's budget would be the most important and most available source of information about what a city does: the ends it serves and the resources it allocates to attain them. In fact, budgets have so far proved to be a poor source of reliable information. Expenditures are differently classified in different cities; functions performed in one city by the general administration are performed in another by an independent board or commission; state and federal grants-in-aid are a large portion of some cities' expenditures and a small portion of others'; and there are great differences in what money will buy (an old, high-density city may spend much more on school construction or police protection and still buy less education or safety than a newer, low-density city, because the costs of equivalent units of such services are functions of, among other things, land values and land uses). Not only is it difficult to know what the figures in budgets mean, but it is problematical whether the budget allows sufficient freedom of action to the politicians to permit them to make any meaningful decisions about resource allocation.[7] Cities are (or think they are) pinched for revenue, so much of which must go for the maintenance of "essential" services that little, if anything, is left over for new programs. (This fact in itself is important, for in principle many of these services are not "essential" in the sense that government must administer them or, if government does administer them, that it must pay for them out of tax revenue. One might have thought that their high degree of local autonomy would have encouraged at least a few cities in America to experiment more than they have with user charges or private management.)

The systematic data on inputs is in only slightly better form. The *Municipal Yearbook,* for example, conceals more than it reveals by its classification of some cities as "partisan" and some as "nonpartisan." (Boston and Chicago are "nonpartisan" in an utterly different sense from Los Angeles or Detroit; many writers have explained why this is so, but there seems as yet to be no way of using better categories for the kind of routine but essential fact-gathering service that the International City Managers' Association performs for us). Election data are in even worse shape. Efforts are now under way to put the collection of local election data on a more systematic basis, but the task that confronts the brave scholars who are trying to effect this change makes the job Richard Scammon did for national and state voting statistics simple by comparison. As long as the citizens of Los Angeles, for example, refuse to accommodate scholars by adopting a small-ward system for tabulating votes, the scholars will have to do electoral analysis by using as the basic unit either one city of 2.5 million or several thousand precincts of a few hundred people each. But at least in Los Angeles you know where the precincts are. In some other large cities, precinct lines change frequently between elections, but nobody in the cities seems to have kept track of what these changes have been.

Even if input and output data could be put into usable form, it is not at all clear what they would show. The most obvious indicators of the quality of life in our cities—per capita income, median school years completed, home ownership, morbidity rates, participation in cultural activities—are not much affected by the form or functioning of city government.[8] The American city is not Aristotle's self-sufficient city-state; the life chances of an American city dweller are much more the function of aggregate national and regional factors (economic growth, the structure of the labor market, national security) than of factors over which local officials and "power structures" have much control. It would be hard to sustain the argument that the distribution of those things *most* important to *most* people is greatly affected by the distribution of power in the community. It is not by any means clear that much can be said even about those things that concern the "attentive elite" in our cities—such as the efficiency of municipal services. The measurement of municipal services has made little progress since Herbert Simon and Clarence Ridley first (unsuccessfully) tried it, the reason being that the services supplied by different cities and the tastes of the consumers in different cities are rarely the same.[9]

In the long run, none of these problems may prove insuperable; and certainly every reasonable effort to develop and refine data sources that are useful in making gross intercity comparisons or helpful as indicators of urban trends ought to be encouraged. Several of my colleagues are energetically pressing the search for gross, "hard data" observables that will make it possible to assert interesting facts about the outcomes of city politics without having, as Norton Long puts it, "to hide under the mayor's bed." It certainly would make for a more efficient and systematic social science of cities if it were possible to answer the important questions by knowing how the data are correlated instead of where the bodies are buried. I am warmly sympathetic to efforts to get the first kind of answers, but I am not optimistic that for the foreseeable future we shall be able to avoid the necessity of disinterring a few political skeletons. A political sociology or even political economy of cities may be the ultimate objective, but a political anthropology is still very much in order.

Input-output analysis in the study of urban politics has made even less progress (if that is possible) than input-output analysis in political science generally. It is still necessary to study the contents of the black box, and not simply to examine what goes in and what comes out. No substitute has yet been found for the intelligent observer who can find the tribal informants and extract from them a rich, complex, and largely subjective account of the lives, values, goals, habits, and methods of the city fathers. We can, however, begin to shift the focus of such research to stress (1) new *objectives* of analysis, (2) new *levels* of analysis, and (3) new *units* of analysis.

The new objectives would emphasize, as I have said before, an effort to explain the outcomes of community politics and government. There are two broad strategies for making this effort. First, one can begin, as Williams and Adrian have done, with a small number of communities that are presumably different in important ways and then seek to understand what differences, if any, in the ends of government action there are among the cities and what aspects of the cities—social, economic, ecological, or political— account for these differences. Finding the differences, though not simple, is of course the easiest part of the investigation. The harder part lies in attributing causation among the enormous number of possible explanations. Solving the problem of identifying the dependent variables (by intensive study of a few com-

138

munities that one hopes will provide different outcomes) makes it that much harder to solve the problem of specifying the independent variables. The second approach is to find some measure of an outcome (for example, the adoption of an urban-renewal or fluoridation program, the level of welfare or educational expenditures, or the crime rate) and apply that measure to a very large number of cities. The familiar techniques of multivariate and regression analysis would then be used to discover what "input" factors are associated with the variation in the dependent variable. The problem with this approach, as I hope I have made clear by now, is that for most of the interesting outputs we have no reliable measures. We have lots of "measures" (like the FBI Uniform Crime Reports, educational expenditures per pupil in average daily attendance, and net project costs for urban-renewal projects completed or authorized), but nobody knows for sure what any of these "measures" measure. The crime rates are the most notoriously unreliable, but the others are not much better. Solving the problem of specifying the independent variables (by having enough cities in our sample to make statistical techniques useful) makes it that much harder to solve the problem of specifying the content of the dependent variables. The seemingly inevitable gains and losses associated with these two research strategies make me think that there is at work in social science an equivalent of the Heisenberg Uncertainty Principle, such that success in determining the magnitude of one variable precludes the possibility of determining the magnitude of another.

The easy (and conventional) way out of this Hobson's choice is to say that the method one picks depends on the questions one wants to answer, and then to change the subject. This is of course true, but it never really works that way. The method one chooses rarely depends simply on what questions one seeks to answer; it really depends on the personal research style of the investigator, almost regardless of what method is theoretically best.[10] Recognizing this, I am willing to go a bit further than the easy answer and suggest that, at this stage, although much bolder experimentation with aggregate-data analysis is needed, real progress still requires the intensive study of a small number of communities. This is so not simply because it happens to be my research style, but also because intensive "outcome-oriented" research is critically necessary to enable us to learn in detail what the "outcomes" are, how they may be measured (if at all), and what factors *seem* to be causally related to them.

The level, as well as the ends, of analysis should be specified. In principle (and to a considerable extent in practice) there are three possible levels: the individual, the group or organization, and the system. I think it fair to say that almost all the research on urban politics done over the last several years has emphasized the second level.[11] One now can refer to a sizable number of respectable studies on urban party organizations, pressure groups, leadership patterns, "power structures," and the like. These organizations or groups or cliques, however, operate within a system, constrained not only by the character of the system as a whole but by the preferences of the individuals (voters, members of voluntary associations, newspaper readers, and party workers) whose dispensation (or indifference) is required before action can be concerted toward organizational or community goals. Much more needs to be done at the organizational level; I would be the last to urge anyone to abandon studies of this sort. All kinds of institutions have received only the sketchiest study—newspapers, the more important voluntary and civic associations, and municipal bureaucracies, to name only three obvious examples. Nevertheless, the great void exists at the other two levels: that of the individual and that of the urban political system as a whole.[12]

I do not say this in order to open up a sterile controversy about reductionism in social science. I know there are always a few scholastics around who insist on pointing out for the twentieth time why one cannot (or can) explain collective behavior as the consequence of individual attributes. The point I want to make is somewhat different: analysis entirely at one structural level (a) makes explanations of the outputs of whole systems unlikely and (b) reduces the possibility of comparative study. It has the first deficiency because it does not take into account the constraints (or, from another perspective, opportunities) facing organizations; it has the second because the study of a single institution or organization almost invariably leads the research deeper and deeper into the organization and farther and farther away from those *gross* characteristics of the organization that distinguish it from others in the same community or indicate its similarity to comparable organizations in other communities. There is no inevitable reason why this should be so except for the very real fact that knowledge tends to come in dissertation-sized chunks; trying to force a graduate student who has learned enough about one organization to satisfy his thesis committee to go out and do the same thing on a similar organization in a different city is widely regarded as an unfair labor practice.

Despite the popularity of survey and electoral research during the last fifteen or twenty years, little of this research has been done on cities. This is not surprising; cities have rarely been the arena in which momentous national issues are fought out. The current civil-rights controversy may change all this. One continuing difficulty, of course, has been that a principal source of funds—the federal government—has not in the past been anxious to sponsor research that had as its major categories ethnicity and religion and that was explicitly directed toward political questions in some congressman's district.

There is reason to believe that some of these constraints will be relaxed or got around. The important thing, however, is to decide what questions are worth asking of local voters. It seems to me that the city is the best place to explore the kinds of attachments citizens have to the polity—their sense of obligation or duty, their conception of the public interest, and the extent to which (or the circumstances in which) their preferences in community programs are the product of rational self-interest or of learned cultural norms.[13] These are difficult questions to answer in any circumstances; but they are doubly so when the question at issue is stated in general terms, resolved in a remote place, and experienced only indirectly—in short, when it is a "momentous national issue." It is the very ordinariness of local concerns—garbage collection, police protection, street repair, school programs—that make them valuable as tools to explore the nature of citizenship and civility. These services are directly experienced, their quality is (in principle) calculable in terms of narrow self-interest, and they are paid for by a variety of interesting tax and revenue procedures that have a very uneven incidence.

Furthermore, survey and electoral analyses done intensively in one or a few cities permit heavy sampling of certain groups that are more thinly dispersed in the national population—Negroes, Italians, Poles, and Jews, for example—and about which our knowledge is largely fragmentary and impressionistic. (Our understanding of middle-class Negroes has not kept pace with our interest in them, in part because they are such tiny portions of random national samples.) Survey research can help us to understand the city in a way that, until now, we have not; but the help will be limited unless some professional constraints are eased. The drive for impeccable technique has progressed at the expense of substantive knowledge, precisely because (among other reasons) the most interesting questions are the most difficult to phrase and code. (One valuable source of survey data about urban politics—the Detroit Area Study—has not fully realized its promise, largely, I think, because it has not asked very interesting questions; and it has not done so, I would guess, in part because the answers to such questions are extraordinarily difficult to handle in a routinized and easily replicable manner.) It has been said before but I will say it again: we need to exploit more fully the techniques of Samuel Lubell and David Riesman before we can decide to what extent the techniques of the Survey Research Center are applicable.

The urban political system is, like the individual, a level of analysis where the need at present is for less rather than more rigor.[14] (The level of organizational analysis is one where *more* rigor—or at least more effort at being systematic—is required.) By "urban political system" I mean something rather simple— for example, in what politically important respects do the growing cities of the Southwest differ from the stagnant or declining cities of the Northeast? What difference to politics do the facts of affluence, a rapid increase in population and land values, and an in-migration of already acculturated, middle-class families (instead of alien, lower-class families) make?[15] What important differences does city size make in the issues that arise and in the manner in which those issues are resolved (or not resolved)?[16] What have been the secular trends for different kinds of cities over the last half-century? (Several fascinating changes suggest themselves, but they have largely been ignored in contemporary research. Not very long ago, in any strike the police were automatically on the side of business; today the police are either neutral or—in some cases—on the side of the unions. Not long ago, known thieves running on pro-thievery platforms could be elected to high municipal office; today, hardly any *known* thieves stand a chance.)

Analyzing urban political systems as systems cannot be done

simply by trying to look at the system "whole," for there are always as many "wholes" as there are observers. Furthermore, it may be that not all of urban politics has the character of a "system"—that is, of a set of interdependent variables. Attention must therefore be given to the appropriate *units* of analysis. Most recently, the unit employed by the political scientist has been the *issue,* and that employed by some (though by no means all) sociologists has been the *elite.* As we all know by now, these differences (among others) have led to different research findings. Looking at issues—i.e., at conflict—one is more likely to find pluralism, contention, and bargaining. Looking for elites, one is more likely to *find* elites (i.e., persons who possess a disproportionate share of some resource, such as income, prestige, or putative power). Having recognized this, I do not feel that truth lies in eclecticism. Using both methods simultaneously may only add the errors of one to the shortcomings of the other. I happen to believe that the issue-oriented approach is, in most circumstances, the most fruitful one—in part because American cities, to a greater extent than cities almost anywhere else, are engaged in managing conflict; in part because many of the crucial features of a system are best seen under conditions of strain and conflict; and in part because asking people who they think is "powerful," no matter how carefully the findings are subsequently validated, is at best a waste of time and at worst misleading.

The real difficulty with the issue-oriented approach is not that it is wrong but that it leaves a great deal unsaid. Some communities produce few, if any, obvious issues.[17] In other communities, certain matters do *not* become issues because some group that can influence the civic agenda manages to suppress certain demands; these "nonissues" may be even more interesting than the problems that do find a place on the agenda.[18] Furthermore, in any city, what is of greatest importance to the daily lives of the

144

citizens and most influential in the conduct of American government as a whole may not be issues at all but may instead be certain services and institutions that are largely taken for granted.

I suggest that the most challenging area for new research on cities is to take as the unit of analysis the routine behavior of the city as it provides certain services or as it conducts its political affairs. Three examples of such units are the system of justice, the educational system, and the welfare system.

The system of justice—and my early research suggests that it *is* a system and not simply a collection of institutions such as courts, prosecutors, and police officers—should be examined as a means by which the community exemplifies and enforces its normative codes. The system of justice, I suspect, is best seen not in the highly publicized murder trial but in the routine disposition of drunks, vagrants, shoplifters, auto thieves, and fornicators.

The problem in examining education is not to justify its importance (that, I take it, is obvious) but to find some way of assessing its output. If professional school administrators cannot tell us how to recognize good as opposed to poor education or how to measure how "much" education we are producing, then political scientists concerned with the outcome of urban governmental arrangements cannot be blamed for avoiding the field for so long.[19] Nonetheless, interesting issues remain. How, and by what criteria, are educational resources allocated among various groups and neighborhoods within the community? How is the distribution of influence within the school system related to the kinds of subjects and the types of students taught? If taxable income and teachable children continue to abandon the central city, what alternatives exist for the management of America's great experiment with mass education under public auspices?

The politics of welfare programs in our cities ought to be broadly conceived, to include not only the conventional forms of

145

public assistance and relief but all measures by which the city government, implicitly or explicitly, seeks to redistribute income. The larger and older central cities are, in some cases, well on their way to becoming the urban equivalents of Indian reservations in which perpetual wards of the state are subsidized by a system of "welfare colonialism" that creates serious problems (e.g., subsidizing broken homes) while solving others (e.g., preventing starvation). We know little of how (or by whom) the goals of these programs are set, how politics intervenes (if at all) in the administration of these programs, or how the level of welfare expenditures differs from city to city. New programs in the welfare field, such as federally sponsored "community action" organizations in lower-class neighborhoods, raise interesting questions about the sort of incentives necessary to mobilize the impoverished; the implications of these incentives for the goals and tactics of the organizations; and the propriety of using public revenues to support a program that, at least in some cities, consists very largely of organized political and civic action directed *against* the governmental institutions that are paying the bill.

Thinking back over all this, I suspect I may have emphasized more than I meant to the need for goal-oriented comparative research on cities. There are, I should like to repeat, many intellectually interesting questions that, if answered, do not necessarily illuminate the question of outcomes. (No one, by the way, has to my knowledge ever proposed a satisfactory set of criteria for distinguishing intellectually interesting from intellectually uninteresting questions. Maybe that is because devising such criteria does not seem intellectually interesting.) Understanding politics, a very difficult subject to comprehend, is intrinsically satisfying; and it needs no other justification than that. I here emphasize the ends of community action, not because there is no other way

146

to do research, but because I feel political science has, in some degree, a peculiar mission and competence: to think simultaneously about the quality of the ends that are served and the reasons why those ends, and not others, are in fact served.[20] But also I feel that a preoccupation with outcomes is the most meaningful way to do comparative research, that it is a preoccupation closest to the subjective states of the principal actors in politics, and that it directs attention to "high stakes" matters rather than "low stakes" matters. Although we have had a number of studies about community conflict that have told us something about how urban renewal or fluoridation programs are enacted or defeated, in the long run these programs may turn out to be trivial, or very nearly so.[21] For most people, the stakes are low (even for the most involved actors, the stakes may be as much the fun of playing a civic game as a real concern with the outcome). Those matters over which the community has any significant control that have high stakes for most of us are few compared to those found at the national level; but they include how our children are educated, how our taxes are levied, how (and to what end) our poor are supported, how the use of our land is controlled, and how (and in whose behalf) our criminal laws are enforced. To a great extent, they include many of the matters that, taken together, make up some significant part of what we mean when we speak of civility. And that, I feel, is not an unworthy subject.

NOTES

1. I will omit the conventional footnote and refer instead to an anthology: Charles Press, ed., *Main Street Politics* (East Lansing, Mich.: Institute for Community Development, 1962).

2. Norton E. Long, "Aristotle and the Study of Local Govern-

ment," in *The Polity* (Chicago: Rand McNally, 1962), pp. 222-41.

3. *Ibid.*, p. 228.

4. Maurice Pinard, "Structural Attachments and Political Support in Urban Politics: The Case of Fluoridation Referendums," *American Journal of Sociology*, March, 1963, pp. 513-26.

5. "Community Power and Urban Renewal Success," *ibid.*, January, 1963, pp. 422-31. Hawley's findings have been challenged in Bruce C. Straits, "Community Adoption and Implementation of Urban Renewal," *ibid.*, July, 1965, pp. 77-82.

6. Oliver P. Williams and Charles R. Adrian, *Four Cities* (Philadelphia: University of Pennsylvania Press, 1963).

7. Cf. the account of budget-making in New York City given in Lillian Ross, "$1,031,961,754.73," in Oliver P. Williams and Charles Press (eds.), *Democracy in Urban America* (Chicago: Rand McNally, 1961), pp. 418-35.

8. Cf. Edward C. Banfield and James Q. Wilson, *City Politics* (Cambridge, Mass.: Harvard University Press, 1963), pp. 329-46.

9. Clarence Ridley and Herbert Simon, *Measuring Municipal Activities* (Chicago: International City Managers' Association, 1938) and Alice Vandermeulen, "Guideposts for Measuring the Efficiency of Governmental Expenditure," *Public Administration Review*, Winter, 1950, pp. 7-12. Recently, renewed attention has been paid to the problems of criteria, as a result of the effort to apply cost-benefit analysis to municipal services. See the papers in Howard G. Schaller, *Public Expenditure Decisions in the Urban Community* (Washington, D.C.: Resources for the Future, 1963).

10. A brilliant account of the meaning of theory and research is Michael Polanyi, *Personal Knowledge* (Chicago: University of Chicago Press, 1958), especially chaps. IV, VI, X.

11. The same point I am here making with respect to urban political studies has been made with respect to organizational theory in Peter M. Blau, "The Comparative Study of Organizations" (paper delivered at the annual meeting of the American Political Science Association, Chicago, September, 1964).

12. There are some conspicuous exceptions. Edward C. Banfield, *Political Influence* (New York: Free Press, 1961) not only analyzes the behavior of some of the principal organizations involved in Chicago politics but discusses the consequences for public policy of

the distribution of influence in the community as a whole. Robert A. Dahl, *Who Governs?* (New Haven: Yale University Press, 1961) combines an analysis of organizations and elites with a study of voter attitudes and political participation. The forthcoming study of southern Negroes by Donald Matthews and James Prothro uses survey and local-informant data in combination to show the relationship between the distribution of attitudes and the level of organizational activity in various communities.

13. Edward C. Banfield and I have explored some of these matters, using data from municipal referenda elections, in "Public-Regardingness as a Value Premise in Voting Behavior," *American Political Science Review,* December, 1964, pp. 876-87. We are now testing some of these hypotheses by means of interviewing.

14. On the subject of comparative urban studies, see the excellent treatment in H. Douglas Price, "Comparative Analysis in State and Local Politics: Potential and Problems" (paper presented before the annual meeting of the American Political Science Association, New York City, September, 1963).

15. *Ibid.,* pp. 17-20, and H. Douglas Price, review of *Who Governs?* in *Yale Law Journal,* July, 1962, especially pp. 1094-95.

16. The subject has been opened up by James G. Coke, "The Lesser Metropolitan Areas of Illinois," *Illinois Government* (published by the Institute of Government and Public Affairs, University of Illinois), no. 15, November, 1962.

17. Cf. Arthur Vidich and Joseph Bensman, *Small Town in Mass Society* (Princeton, N.J.: Princeton University Press, 1958), chap. V-VIII, and James S. Coleman, *Community Conflict* (Glencoe, Ill.: Free Press, 1959).

18. See Peter Bachrach and Morton S. Baratz, "Decisions and Nondecisions: An Analytical Framework," *American Political Science Review,* September, 1963, pp. 632-42, especially pp. 641-42, and Banfield, *Political Influence,* pp. 9-10.

19. A fruitful beginning was made almost thirty years ago; but, until the Syracuse studies were begun, no one tried to follow it up. See Nelson B. Henry and Jerome G. Kerwin, *Schools and City Government* (Chicago: University of Chicago Press, 1938).

20. The current functionalist approach to comparative government has recently been criticized, in a similar way, for failing to use

policy as an explicit variable: Roy Pierce, "Comparative Politics: Liberty and Policy as Variables," *American Political Science Review*, September, 1963, pp. 655-60.

21. This does not mean that nothing significant can be learned from such issues. Two important "single city" studies have been done on urban-renewal politics: Peter Rossi and Robert Dentler, *The Politics of Urban Renewal: The Chicago Findings* (New York: Free Press, 1961) and Harold Kaplan, *Urban Renewal Politics: Slum Clearance in Newark* (New York: Columbia University Press, 1963).